14.95

**HOW TO SAY IT**

# Doing Business in Latin America

## A Pocket Guide to the Culture, Customs, and Etiquette

D1015979

## Kevin Michael Diran, EdD

PRENTICE HALL PRESS

PRENTICE HALL PRESS
Published by the Penguin Group
Penguin Group (USA) Inc.
375 Hudson Street, New York, New York 10014, USA
Penguin Group (Canada), 90 Eglinton Avenue East, Suite 700, Toronto,
Ontario M4P 2Y3, Canada (a division of Pearson Penguin Canada Inc.) •
Penguin Books Ltd., 80 Strand, London WC2R 0RL, England • Penguin
Group Ireland, 25 St. Stephen's Green, Dublin 2, Ireland (a division of
Penguin Books Ltd.) • Penguin Group (Australia), 250 Camberwell Road,
Camberwell, Victoria 3124, Australia (a division of Pearson Australia
Group Pty. Ltd.) • Penguin Books India Pvt. Ltd., 11 Community Centre,
Panchsheel Park, New Delhi—110 017, India • Penguin Group (NZ),
67 Apollo Drive, Rosedale, North Shore 0632, New Zealand (a division
of Pearson New Zealand Ltd.) • Penguin Books (South Africa) (Pty.) Ltd.,
24 Sturdee Avenue, Rosebank, Johannesburg 2196, South Africa

Penguin Books Ltd., Registered Offices: 80 Strand, London WC2R 0RL,
England

While the author has made every effort to provide accurate telephone
numbers and Internet addresses at the time of publication, neither the
publisher nor the author assumes any responsibility for errors, or for
changes that occur after publication. Further, the publisher does not
have any control over and does not assume any responsibility for author
or third-party websites or their content.

First edition: September 2009

Library of Congress Cataloging-in-Publication Data

Diran, Kevin Michael.
   How to say it : doing business in Latin America : a pocket guide to the
culture, customs and etiquette / Kevin Michael Diran.
       p.   cm.
   Includes bibliographical references and index.
   ISBN 978-0-7352-0443-0
  1. Business etiquette—Latin America.   2. Corporate culture—Latin
America.   3. Business communication—Latin America.   4. Intercultural
communication—Latin America.   5. Latin America—Social life and
customs.   I. Title.
   HF5389.3.L3D57 2009
   395.5'2098—dc22                                         2009018921

PRINTED IN THE UNITED STATES OF AMERICA

10  9  8  7  6  5  4  3  2  1

Most Prentice Hall Press books are available at special quantity discounts
for bulk purchases for sales promotions, premiums, fund-raising, or
educational use. Special books, or book excerpts, can also be created to fit
specific needs. For details, write: Special Markets, Penguin Group (USA)
Inc., 375 Hudson Street, New York, New York 10014.

*I dedicate this book to the incomparable Carol Egan,
who, as wife, playmate, lover,
consultant, traveling companion and literary
critic, proved to be of invaluable assistance
in the writing of this book.*

# Acknowledgments

All books are the product of a team effort, although only the author has a name on the cover. The production of this book required the input of my Latin American *amigos* who have opened to me their hearts, minds, homes and businesses.

Without the encouragement, patience and hard work of Maria Gagliano, my editor at Penguin, this book would never have been written. Her mark is upon every line. Managing editor Jennifer Eck and copyeditor Rick Willett had the unenviable task of polishing the text into something readable.

Literary agent Lilly Ghahremani of Full Circle Literary in San Diego was invaluable in providing the kind of professional support and guidance that could serve as a role model for literary agents everywhere.

# Contents

# Foreword

Congratulations for having the courage to take on an exciting new venture. You are about to enter Latin America, which may be a foreign cultural environment for you. We all know that there can be no good business without good communications. The importance of your English-speaking skills and sensibilities, so valuable to you during your business career, will account for little in this novel environment. The language will naturally constitute a communications barrier, but more significantly, the other barriers, in terms of economic, social, educational and cultural differences, can present even greater challenges in achieving your business objectives, whether they be selling or purchasing. These are the challenges we will address in this book.

Latin American business culture is constructed on personal relationships. Without these connections, there is little chance for success. As an English-speaking person, your challenge is to build relationships with executives who speak a different language and have been inculcated with a different set of values.

Latin American business culture is in part also characterized by its systemic corruption. Finding ways to maneuver through this byzantine system is daunting. Your greatest challenge may be finding the patience needed to conquer what might seem to be a prevailing

sense of procrastination. Of course, you will learn that
it is not really procrastination, but rather a cultural difference. Generally speaking, in Latin America, no great
value is attached to speed or efficiency.

At the end of this book, you'll find yourself traveling
through the Latin American cultural landscape with relative ease. A sense of security, which comes from accurate knowledge concerning the world you are entering,
will sustain you.

# Introduction

*All journeys have secret destinations of
which the traveler is unaware.*
—Martin Buber

It has been a long, hot day and tomorrow you are heading home. The company's first Latin American contract is in your briefcase. Settling in the café that you discovered when you first arrived, the question of the moment is *Should I order a Corona or a margarita?* It is time to take stock, look back and pat yourself on the back. You did it. So, was it worth it? Certainly. Was it fun? Sometimes. Was it easy? No. Sailing into uncharted waters is never easy.

*How do I obtain my initial introduction, which is vitally important? How do I communicate when I do not have adequate command of the language? How do I move around in an unfamiliar environment? How do I avoid expensive delays? Where do I find the assistance I need?* These are common concerns, and if you are anxious to succeed and do a brilliant job, stick with the techniques in this book. I will explore the common challenges you may run into and provide tips on the right buttons to push with your new business associates. You'll learn the ins and outs on traveling and doing business in fascinating but unfamiliar territory where lifestyles are so very different.

U.S. Merchandise Trade with Selected
Latin American Countries and Groups, 1996–2007

| Country | 1996 | 1998 | 2000 | 2002 | 2004 | 2006 | 2007 | % Change 2006–2007 | % Change 1996–2007 |
|---|---|---|---|---|---|---|---|---|---|
| | | | | | | | | | U.S. EXPORTS ($ BILLIONS) |
| **Brazil** | 12.7 | 15.2 | 15.4 | 12.4 | 13.9 | 19.2 | 24.6 | 28.1% | 93.7% |
| **Venezuela** | 4.8 | 6.5 | 5.6 | 4.5 | 4.8 | 9.0 | 10.2 | 13.3% | 112.5% |
| **Colombia** | 4.7 | 4.8 | 3.7 | 3.6 | 4.5 | 6.7 | 8.6 | 28.4% | 83.0% |
| **Chile** | 4.1 | 4.0 | 3.5 | 2.6 | 3.6 | 6.8 | 8.3 | 22.1% | 102.4% |
| **Dom. Rep.** | 3.2 | 4.0 | 4.4 | 4.3 | 4.4 | 5.4 | 6.1 | 13.0% | 90.6% |
| **Argentina** | 4.5 | 5.9 | 4.7 | 1.6 | 3.4 | 4.8 | 5.9 | 22.9% | 31.1% |
| **Costa Rica** | 1.8 | 2.3 | 2.4 | 3.1 | 3.3 | 4.1 | 4.6 | 12.2% | 155.6% |
| **Honduras** | 1.6 | 2.3 | 2.6 | 2.6 | 3.1 | 3.7 | 4.5 | 21.6% | 181.3% |
| **Guatemala** | 1.6 | 1.9 | 1.9 | 2.0 | 2.6 | 3.5 | 4.1 | 17.1% | 156.3% |
| **Peru** | 1.8 | 2.1 | 1.7 | 1.6 | 2.1 | 2.9 | 4.1 | 41.4% | 127.8% |
| **Other** | 11.7 | 14.4 | 13.4 | 13.4 | 21.4 | 22.9 | 26.5 | 15.7% | 126.5% |
| **Total LAC*** | 52.5 | 63.4 | 59.3 | 51.7 | 61.5 | 89.0 | 107.5 | 20.8% | 104.8% |
| **Mexico** | 56.8 | 79.0 | 111.0 | 97.5 | 110.8 | 134.2 | 136.1 | 1.4% | 139.6% |
| **Total Lat. Amer.** | 109.3 | 142.4 | 171.0 | 149.2 | 172.3 | 223.2 | 243.6 | 9.1% | 122.9% |
| **CAFTA–DR** | 9.6 | 12.4 | 13.6 | 14.1 | 15.8 | 19.6 | 22.4 | 14.3% | 133.3% |
| **Caricom** | 4.4 | 5.0 | 5.4 | 5.0 | 5.8 | 8.6 | 9.2 | 7.0% | 109.1% |
| **Mercosur** | 18.6 | 22.4 | 21.0 | 14.6 | 18.2 | 25.4 | 32.4 | 27.6% | 74.2% |
| **Andean Comm.** | 12.8 | 15.5 | 12.2 | 11.4 | 13.2 | 21.6 | 26.1 | 20.8% | 103.9% |
| **World** | 625.1 | 680.5 | 780.4 | 693.1 | 818.8 | 1,037.1 | 1,162.5 | 12.1% | 86.0% |

| Country | 1996 | 1998 | 2000 | 2002 | 2004 | 2006 | 2007 | % Change 2006–2007 | % Change 1996–2007 |
|---|---|---|---|---|---|---|---|---|---|
| | | | | | | | | | U.S. IMPORTS ($ BILLIONS) |
| Brazil | 8.8 | 10.1 | 13.9 | 15.8 | 21.2 | 26.4 | 25.6 | -3.0% | 190.9% |
| Venezuela | 12.9 | 9.3 | 18.7 | 15.1 | 24.9 | 37.2 | 39.9 | 7.3% | 209.3% |
| Colombia | 4.3 | 4.7 | 7.0 | 5.6 | 7.3 | 9.3 | 9.4 | 1.1% | 118.6% |
| Chile | 2.3 | 2.5 | 3.2 | 3.8 | 4.7 | 9.5 | 9.0 | -5.3% | 291.3% |
| Dom. Rep. | 3.6 | 4.4 | 4.4 | 4.2 | 4.5 | 4.5 | 4.2 | -6.7% | 16.7% |
| Argentina | 2.3 | 2.3 | 3.1 | 3.2 | 3.8 | 4.0 | 4.5 | 12.5% | 95.7% |
| Costa Rica | 2.0 | 2.8 | 3.6 | 3.1 | 3.3 | 3.8 | 3.9 | 2.6% | 95.0% |
| Honduras | 1.8 | 2.6 | 3.1 | 3.3 | 3.7 | 3.7 | 3.9 | 5.4% | 116.7% |
| Guatemala | 1.7 | 2.1 | 2.6 | 2.8 | 3.2 | 3.1 | 3.0 | -3.2% | 76.5% |
| Peru | 1.3 | 2.0 | 2.0 | 1.9 | 3.7 | 5.9 | 5.3 | -10.2% | 307.7% |
| Other | 7.8 | 7.6 | 11.7 | 10.8 | 18.4 | 26.3 | 26.1 | -0.8% | 234.6% |
| Total LAC* | 48.8 | 50.4 | 73.3 | 69.6 | 98.7 | 133.7 | 134.8 | 0.8% | 176.2% |
| Mexico | 74.3 | 94.7 | 135.9 | 134.7 | 155.9 | 198.3 | 210.7 | 6.3% | 183.6% |
| Total Lat. Amer. | 123.1 | 145.1 | 209.2 | 204.3 | 254.6 | 332.0 | 345.5 | 4.1% | 180.7% |
| CAFTA-DR | 10.4 | 13.7 | 16.1 | 16.0 | 17.7 | 18.6 | 18.7 | 0.5% | 79.8% |
| Caricom | 2.9 | 2.6 | 4.0 | 4.0 | 7.7 | 10.4 | 11.0 | 5.8% | 279.3% |
| Mercosur | 11.4 | 12.6 | 17.3 | 19.2 | 25.5 | 30.9 | 30.7 | -0.6% | 169.3% |
| Andean Comm. | 21.1 | 17.8 | 30.0 | 24.9 | 40.4 | 59.8 | 61.1 | 2.2% | 189.6% |
| World | 795.3 | 913.9 | 1,216.9 | 1,161.4 | 1,469.7 | 1,855.1 | 1,957.0 | 5.5% | 146.1% |

**Source:** Table created by CRS from U.S. Department of Commerce data.
*LAC = Latin America and the Caribbean, except Mexico.

The Latin American economy is, in general, booming, with a population of more than 500 million people and increasing trade with the United States. It is a great place to sell, source and outsource. There will be profitable repeat business. Moreover, even though you must deal with cultural differences, these challenges are far less daunting than you would face in doing business in other parts of the world, and are sure to produce rewarding results.

An examination of the chart prepared by the Congressional Research Service, which is created from U.S. Department of Commerce data (below), shows which countries are trading and their percentages of increase from 1996 to 2007, which is the last year for which verifiable data is available. United States–to–Latin American exports increased 20.8 percent in 2006–2007, and total Latin American trade from the United States increased 176.2 percent between 1996 and 2007. This is to say that business between the United States and Latin America is booming.

Note that at the bottom of the chart we are given breakdowns for the various free trade communities in which the United States participates in both Latin and Central America. Notice the higher trade statistics for countries who participate in these agreements:

CAFTA with the Dominican Republic, which is a Caribbean country.

CARICOM with Belize, which is a Central American country.

MERCOSUR with Argentina, Brazil, Paraguay and Uruguay

Andean Community with Bolivia, Colombia, Ecuador
and Peru

The difficulty of the task facing you is determined by
several factors:

1. If you have corporate support on the ground in
   Latin America, your way will be smoother than if
   you are an independent businessperson depending
   entirely on your own resources. Your local Latin
   American corporate office can supply a plethora of
   the services discussed in this book, in the arenas of
   communications, introductions and trade information as well as the more mundane aspects of travel
   in a foreign country.

2. If you are buying merchandise or services rather
   than selling them, you will have an easier task, as
   lapses are ignored for a person with dollars to spend.
   Sellers face the sometimes difficult task of integrat-
   ing themselves into the culture and making friends
   before any business can be discussed.

3. Some countries are easier business environments
   than others, for political and economic reasons discussed in this book. Mexico, Chile, Uruguay, Brazil and
   Argentina tend to be relatively easy places for Americans to do business, while Colombia, Bolivia, Paraguay and Venezuela tend to pose more challenges.

## COMMUNICATION BASICS

The English language is utilized as the basis for international
trade. English supplanted French as the international lan-

guage shortly after World War II. It was a gradual process, although fragments of French remain. For example, your passport contains a statement in French indicating that you are a citizen of the United States.

The requirement that all international aircraft pilots communicate with traffic controllers only in English perhaps marked the beginning of the transformation. The change was solidified by the fact that the world's financial resources came to be held in English-speaking banks, who are loath to translate millions of commercial documents from a variety of languages into English. This, coupled with the historic lack of necessity for English-speaking peoples to become bilingual, solidified English as the language of trade. For example, a Chinese businessperson in Latin America possessing about as much Spanish as the average American businessperson will generally resort to English or utilize a translator if one can be found. The exception to this English-language-only usage is the rare businessperson who comes from a bilingual background or who has undergone a language-immersion program such as those offered by the U.S. government.

Of course, you can use your Spanish if you have a working knowledge of the language. It would be ideal for you to possess a facile use of idiomatic Latin American Spanish, as this would provide a commanding advantage in your interactions. Unfortunately, a few years of textbook Spanish will not prove adequate in the business context and should not be relied upon. However, speaking a few key phrases in Spanish with a sheepish "I'm trying to learn Spanish but I'm not doing very well" will go a long way toward your acceptance. Smile and they will effusively congratulate you and tell you that you are doing a wonderful job, regardless of your skill level. With that, you'll have taken your first step on the road to success. A basic list of useful Spanish business terms is included in Appendix A.

## HOW TO USE THIS BOOK

This book has been arranged to take you through the process from obtaining an appointment, to securing a contract, to making return visits. In between, I will give you hard-earned advice on the fine art of properly communicating with our neighbors to the south. In short order, your Latin American peers will graciously accept you into their business circle. Nothing pleases your foreign business friends more than seeing you try hard to do things their way.

The differences between our cultures are substantial and cannot be ignored if you are intent upon success. Latin American business culture is complex but can be assimilated when you understand the rationale. The Latin American lifestyle and work ethic are quite a pleasant departure from our harried and impersonal business environment. No, their afternoon siesta is not a time for all to snooze, but rather it may be the occasion for a leisurely two-hour business lunch, or *comida*, during which relationships will be established and business will probably never be discussed. Here time is not money.

In this book you will be introduced to the various styles of doing business in Latin America, a place where events definitely can unfold at an excruciatingly leisurely pace. Patience is something you will come to value as Latin Americans do. With this realization, you will find that the people here are friendly, open and happy to do business with their stateside visitor.

However, your patience may be sorely tested. For example, a close business partner of mine, who was a senior manager, did not show up for a meeting. His mother-in-law was sick, so he stayed home to help the family. Not notified of this cancellation until I arrived for the meeting, I was upset, until I remembered that the Latin American mind-set always puts family before business. We may know that this "family first" attitude is theoretically correct for all of us, but it can be most inconvenient when actually implemented. Relax, there is always *mañana*. Understanding this culture, anticipating such impediments and providing for this sort of eventuality are part of your game plan. Just go with the flow and sortie out for a nice long *comida*. Life is good.

The information outlined in this book grows out of both my eight years of living, working and teaching in Latin America as well as an intensive examination of the literature on the topic. It also incorporates the varied experiences of my "affinity circle" (a concept we'll discuss in Chapter 1) as well as those of other business travelers and Latin American businesspeople who have been my associates, business partners and friends over the years.

Always remember that you are not in a foreign country but rather you are a foreigner in someone else's country and an object of curiosity. You are the person with the strange habits and incomprehensible mannerisms. The extent to which you overcome the Latin American perception of your behavior as strange is the extent to which you will be successful.

Most important, in this book you will learn how to establish a close relationship with Latin American business friends whose trust and respect you will come to earn, and perhaps, in due time, with their many associates.

To enhance usability, this guide is divided into two parts. In the first part, we will cover the general cultural characteristics evident throughout Latin America. The second part contains information specific to each country as well as pointing out any variations from the general cultural themes. I recommend that you complete Part One in its entirety and then move on to Part Two to discover information about the countries that are of special interest. Remember that the information in Part One pertains to all Latin American countries and is not repeated in Part Two.

You will soon be on the inside track to business success in Latin America.

Good luck and be safe.

—Dr. Kevin Michael Diran

**PART 1**

# The Culture

In the first half of this book, we will consider the Latin American business culture in a general sense. The topics discussed here are valid throughout the region, although perhaps expressed in slightly different intensities. Every country is formal by North American standards, although there might be small cultural differences in how that formality is displayed, depending on your location. You might find a tie loosened in Paraguay but not in Uruguay or Costa Rica.

The pace of business is slow, as we'll explore in this first half, which is not to say you might not encounter a rare company that has been taken over by a gang of gung-ho MBAs with a distinctly North American attitude. These companies are not the norm, however, and encountering one should not be part of your business expectations.

We'll also take a look at the system of affinity circles, which is showing some strain under pressure from the multinational corporations entering the business culture in large urban areas, but remains essentially intact. Little importance may be given to affinity circles in years to come, but you are going to Latin America now. Future changes should not affect your current attitudes.

There is corruption in Latin American business, but that too varies by country, with Costa Rica and Uruguay being relatively close to North American cultural standards in this regard. Such countries are the exceptions, however, as we'll see in the chapters ahead.

# 1
# Making the Vital Contact

*Travelers never think that* they *are the foreigners.*
—Mason Cooley

Your initial acceptance by potential business associates is only facilitated through your business connections. It is virtually impossible to successfully initiate business in Latin America without a personal reference or other form of introduction. Strangers, particularly foreigners, are viewed with distrust until they are vetted. Unless you can say, "I know Licenciado Gómez, whom you know," "We are both Rotarians," or something in a like vein, you have slim chances of getting anything more than a courtesy hearing. (Note that *licenciado*, which is commonly abbreviated as *Lic.*, is the ubiquitous title used before the name of an individual who has earned a college degree. This topic is covered in detail on page 66.)

## THE IMPORTANCE OF AFFINITY CIRCLES

Affinity circles are one of the cornerstones of the Latin American business and social structure. The necessity of being perceived as a member of an affinity circle cannot be overemphasized. Unless you are fortunate enough to have a direct personal introduction to your prospective clients, some research will be required to establish a connection to them.

If you are unaware of anyone who knows your prospective client, no matter how remotely, before you leave home do some research to find a professional or personal biography that can provide some point of reference. Research your local associations and even sister city relationships. No connection is too inconsequential for the initial connection.

The six best types of affinity circles, listed in rough order of effectiveness, are:

• **Friends of Friends.** These can be either business or social. Someone your potential client knows and has done business with can provide the optimal recommendation. Before trying to set up an initial appointment, ask this mutual acquaintance to telephone or write to your prospective client suggesting that it would be in his benefit to meet with you. Making this connection will help you overcome the first major hurdle. Even if your domestic contact only vaguely remembers your potential client from a meeting they both attended ten years previously, mention that person in your initial approach.

• **Consulates.** If a direct introduction isn't possible, a potential client's consulate can provide a gold mine of information when you're doing your research. Even if you have a direct introduction before you embark, talk to the commercial attachés at the local consulate for the country or countries you are visiting. Tell them about your business and travel plans and ask them to recommend people you should contact, as this will supplement your initial direct introduction. If you do not have a direct introduction, this type of recommendation, while less potent, might be your only option. If you fail to secure this information from the first person you speak with, try talking to someone else at the consulate. Be persistent.

Even if you have to travel some distance to the consulate branch nearest you, go in person and dress for the part. If you make this effort, you will eventually be able to make the initial contact with your potential client, before making your trip, with an approach such as "Sr. Romez, a friend of yours from the consulate in New York," whom your prospect either actually knows or will try to remember, "asked me to be in touch with you concerning this matter." This represents you to the client as a member of Sr. Romez's circle of business friends, which is true to at least a certain extent. You can use this approach with any number of people recommended to you by the consulates. Latin Americans take courtesy very seriously, and your potential client would think it rude not to follow through on a request from a mutual friend.

To find the location of these consulates as well as an incredible amount of unbiased up-to-date information concerning the country you are visiting, look at *The CIA World Factbook* (www.cia.gov). Not the typical public relations Pollyanna hype, the site offers some unique perspectives. It is for real.

• **Business, Fraternal, Religious, Academic and Professional Organizations.** Your membership in the local chapter of Rotary, Lions, Masons or the like can provide an excellent opening into Latin American affinity circles. If you belong to one of these fraternal organizations, find the contact for the local chapter at your Latin American destination and notify them that you will be visiting on a specific date to attend one of their meetings. Discuss your business as part of the introductory process, and the association officer might volunteer to invite people of interest for you to that meeting. He might even ask you to address the group. If you are lucky, you may find an appropriate contact there. More likely, as you speak to other locals attending the meeting, they will offer to introduce you to the right people for you to visit. This mutual help process among the membership is central to the purpose of such organizations.

Depending on the specific country, the Latin American population is between 50 and 95 percent Catholic. Many Latin Americans belong to Catholic organizations. If you belong to such a group at home, make sure you schedule to attend a meeting at your destination, where you will be warmly welcomed and incorporated into the circle. This is particularly true if you notify the group in advance concerning your attendance.

There are some very active evangelical groups in Latin America, but they have not coalesced to any great extent. A number of small but influential Jewish communities also exist, including twenty-one Orthodox and two Conservative synagogues in Mexico City with a total membership of forty thousand.

Your initial meeting with any of the aforementioned organizations may or may not help business on your current trip. However, attending meetings when you are in a client's country will help you make contacts and secure appointments for the trip that will soon follow. You will be building relationships and making friends.

Many Latin American professionals at the managerial level were educated in the United States. Being alumni of the same school is an excellent connection. Check with your alumni association to see if you share an alma mater with any of your prospective clients.

• *Tocayo.* Your "namesake" constitutes the affinity circle of "last resort." This connection makes the least amount of sense to North Americans. A *tocayo* is someone who shares your first name and therefore shares your saint's day. The assigned feast day of your saint is celebrated in Latin America as a minor second birthday. "My name is John and your name is Juan so we are *tocayos.*" This alone establishes a relationship and is the occasion for smiles and back pounding. If you have a Christian first name, look up your saint's feast day and remember it. This is not very useful until after you have made initial contact with your potential client. It is more of a conversational gambit upon your first face-to-face meeting.

One day while driving in Querétaro, Mexico, I noticed a business sign for "Kevin's Salón de Belleza" (beauty parlor). I went in, introduced myself, and was treated as a long lost relative. Sr. Kevin served coffee and conversation ensued.

Take advantage of this type of connection. The correct salutation on a person's saint day is *"Felicidades por tu santo."* Use *santa* if you're addressing a woman. You have a list of your contacts. Look up their saint's day and record it in your calendar. Send a message on that day offering best wishes. You will be perceived as a *simpático* and cultured person. It is a great excuse for a contact. Your competition is probably unaware of this celebration. Go for it!

Without some sort of introduction or connection, emanating either from your home base or your Latin American destination, no matter how tenuous it might be, you will be at a severe business disadvantage in the Latin American marketplace. Look around, be creative and get a connection.

Affinity circles are, of course, conceptual constructs and do not necessarily meet formally. They are groups of people who know and trust one another and consider themselves friends on one level or another. Those available may occasionally enjoy a lunch together, or they may not. It may be strictly business, but more usually the circle involves socializing for *comida*, holidays and other events. You may not ever know the full extent of your client's affinity group, so be careful of what you say, as word can travel quickly within groups.

Your first encounter with a member of an affinity circle will probably be at a *comida* during which business is not discussed and to which your client has invited a friend or a group of friends. When your host introduces you, he may say (likely in Spanish) something like "My friends, this is my good friend (watch for the words *mi amigo*, or *amiga* if you are a woman) from the United States who is down here representing XYZ, which produces W." You can then join in on the conversation, respond to their inquiries, which may be copious, and attempt to make the best impression you can (more advice on social gatherings can be found in Chapter 7). If you spot a possible prospect as the meal ends, you can quietly ask him if he would like to meet with you and discuss business. Keep it very low-key so as not to embarrass your host if for some reason the prospective client declines your offer.

You will soon build your own affinity circle with other businesspeople who are attached to still other circles. It becomes—in modern parlance—viral.

The main difference between such gatherings in Latin America and in the United States lies in the fact that in Latin America prospective clients are unlikely to be open to anyone who is not introduced by a trusted friend.

Beware. Relationships with your Latin American counterparts can be double-edged swords. If you mess up or disappoint, word of this transgression will spread with amazing speed throughout the Latin American business community and you will have a serious and perhaps fatal business problem. By the same token, once you do the work and are integrated into your client's circle, you can call upon the individuals in that circle as references to secure additional business from other circles. Breaking in is the major challenge, but once you do, it will help you build even more relationships.

## MAKING THE INITIAL CONTACT

Your initial contact with a prospective client will set the tone for much of your communications with him. If you are traveling with corporate support, your prospective client will have been identified for you and an appointment scheduled by someone known to your client. Therefore finding a prospect and introducing yourself should go rather easily. If you are the sole representative for your company, it becomes more complex because you must personally establish a connection with your potential client and make the initial contact through your own devices (ideally through one of the affinity circles mentioned earlier).

After identifying your potential client, it is necessary to establish communications prior to your trip. Choosing the correct method for contacting your prospect is key. Aside from the optimal direct personal face-to-face introduction by a mutual acquaintance, which might not be available, you are left with the conundrum of choosing the best in a series of increasingly unattractive communication alternatives. The question is, What's the best way to initiate contact from your office and later reinforce your nascent relationship with effective follow-up?

## Personal Communications

A major difference between American and Latin American culture is that Latin Americans prefer to do business on a personal level and have a subtly negative attitude toward remote communications. Relationships are established and enriched face-to-face. There are really no exceptions to this rule, and its importance cannot be overemphasized. Remote communications are only useful when absolutely necessary, for example, for setting up an appointment after a mutual acquaintance has recommended you meet. This reality can be frustrating since telephone, fax and electronic communications are undoubtedly faster, cheaper and more convenient, but they will not produce the desired results when conducting business with Latin American clients.

When you do have a face-to-face encounter, you will enjoy your client's complete, undivided attention and highest priority while sitting in front of him, which is wonderful. However, his attention will remain focused on you only until you leave the office. Then your priority evaporates and is assigned to the next person coming in. To a greater or lesser extent, you're forgotten, which is not so wonderful. This is not a collective form of Latin American ADD, but rather a cultural characteristic. Appreciate this characteristic, because it requires an appropriate personal response on your part.

The only way to effectively combat this inattention, impractical as it may seem, is to reappear in front of your prospective client within a few weeks of your first visit and then reappear repeatedly until a strong relationship is established. His trust will be secured as a function of your reliability and accessibility. He will not do business with a cipher. Therefore, it will be necessary to periodically reinforce these relationships, since they have a short shelf life. Repeated visits will eventually help you develop a friendship and the tacit understanding that you will "be there" for each other, which is the foundation of not only a Latin American business relationship, but a business relationship anywhere. This is a hard reality for many North Americans to internalize, because visiting Latin America is a time-consuming and expensive process due to the distances involved.

Once you have established a relationship, securing repeated appointments will not present a problem, because you will have become a visiting friend. Eventually you may not even need an appointment. Perhaps the best type of visit is of the "say hello" variety, which should always occur when you are in the area visiting with another client. Check on your client's business situation, family well-being, World Cup expectations or any connections you have established during your previous trips. These visits help reinforce a relationship. If the client's business is critical to your success, you must do whatever is necessary to secure it, and if this involves multiple face-to-face encounters, so be it.

Is it worth it? That is up to you to decide. The sales process is extended and expensive. What are the potential benefits to you in the short run? In the long run? Although the profits for many competing in this marketplace are substantial, do you have the stamina to carry the process through to completion? Individuals who are not willing to make a commitment of this magnitude are unlikely to enjoy success. If you consider these visits burdensome, it will show.

## Remote Communications

A major problem that foreign businesspeople face in Latin America is the fact that remote communication is not very effective. Anyone who believes otherwise is not likely to succeed. Unfortunately, there are times when circumstances forbid face-to-face communication and you must select the least unappealing alternative for your purpose. If you have no choice but to use them, the major forms of remote communication are the postal service, email, fax and international delivery services. The issues with these communications include uncertain delivery and lack of attention by your client. With the exception of international delivery services—and even they are suspect—there are really no good forms of remote communication with your Latin American client. Here they are discussed from the least to the more effective:

• **Postal Service.** Forget about it! It is slow and unreliable. I have Latin American friends who have been in business for thirty years and have never mailed anything. Mail is often stolen, misdirected or just dumped. Just about everyone in Latin America uses an office messenger to run around town on a motorcycle to make mail deliveries. Anyone who has been unfortunate enough to try to utilize the postal service has his own litany of horror tales.

- **Email** is fast and reasonably reliable in the large urban areas. However, the all-encompassing character- istics of the Internet are not nearly as pervasive in Latin American business as they are in other parts of the world. Young professionals in Latin America are far more likely to respond than are their seniors. Generally speaking, emails are either deleted or put into an electronic "slush file" while your client attends to other matters, so this is not a very effective way to communicate, particularly for an initial introduction. The consignment of emails from unknown parties to the recycle bin without actually reading them is a very common practice. In many cases, the communications are intercepted by secretaries who ignore them as if they were junk mail. It is easy to ignore something as ephemeral and impersonal as an email.

When you are forced to use email, as we sometimes are, you can reinforce the message with a prior telephone call informing your associate that you are sending a com- munication. You will probably only get a secretary on the line and, as it would be truly exceptional to encoun- ter an English-speaking secretary anywhere in Latin America, this task might be best handled by a Spanish speaker, if available. Thirty minutes after sending your email, call again to verify receipt of your message. If you get a secretary again, ask her to verify with her boss that the communication has been received.

• **Fax** is a marginally better alternative than email or the postal service. At least there is a piece of paper on the client's desk, which cannot be eliminated with a Delete key. As with email, it would be best to alert your client by telephone to an impending fax and to call again after transmission, to verify receipt of the document.

• **Telephone.** Among older professionals in Latin America there is a subtle unease about the use of the telephone for business purposes. The technology is adequate, but not lovingly embraced. The exception being among the chattering hordes of teenagers seen parading the malls, each with a cell phone glued to an ear. This is a generational phenomenon, and the attitude of unease will undoubtedly change as these younger generations mature and enter the workplace.

It is optimal to precede your telephone call with either a fax or an email or both on the previous day, scheduling your call and thanking your client in advance for his time. Indicating in this communication your membership in one or more affinity groups would go a long way toward encouraging your client to accept the call. If you promise to make a call on a particular day and at a certain time, do so. Missing your telephone appointment would be considered disrespectful. As with scheduling a meeting, the best time is probably between 11 a.m. and 2 p.m., Monday through Friday. But remember the time differences if you are calling from another zone.

If you can reach your potential client on the telephone for an initial contact, it will permit a language assessment to help determine whether or not you will require a translator for subsequent contact. Your prospective client may be proud of his English skills, but a facile command of a hundred-word English vocabulary may not be adequate for a business transaction. The same goes for you and your Spanish. Sometimes it's difficult to assess a client's skill level, and this difficulty may affect how you decide to communicate. A client saying yes at the appropriate times on the opposite end of the phone line does not automatically indicate that he understands a word you are saying.

Even if your client speaks passable English, his secretaries and receptionists may not. It is frustrating to be on the receiving end of a rapid-fire barrage of idiomatic Spanish and not understand a word of it. Excuse yourself with a *discúlpame por favor, no hablo español* (I'm sorry, I don't speak Spanish) and hang up. Find someone to initiate the call for you in Spanish but speak to the client yourself when you eventually reach the person.

Your chances for effective communication after a telephone call will increase if followed by written communication either by fax or email or both. The purpose would be to reconfirm the telephone discussion and repeat any significant points that had been made.

• **International Delivery Services.** This is by far the best choice for your written communications, both to and within a particular country. It has fewer disadvantages than the other methodologies listed above, in that professionally it is harder to ignore than the other forms of remote communication. Important communications come through international delivery services, and so by association your message becomes important. Keep the following guidelines in mind when using this approach:

- Keep your communication brief, with simple and short sentences.
- Use the best-quality paper you can with an embossed letterhead.
- Say who you are, including your title and company name.
- Avoid the word "sales" if you can, as it is perceived negatively.
- Say who recommended you and send his regards to your prospective client.
- Give a very brief indication of your business. Vagueness is preferred over precision, as it will not provide an easy excuse to decline your initiative.
- Remember to include an indication of your academic credentials in your closing, as indicated in Chapter 3 where we discuss the significance of academic credentials.
- Include a copy of your Spanish-language business card.
- Say you will contact the prospective client's office by telephone to secure an appointment. Do so the day after you receive a receipt of delivery. Do not be even a bit tardy in this matter. It may take several tries to reach your client. If you have a Spanish speaker within reach, have that person make the part of the call necessary to get past the typically Spanish-speaking secretary.

For international delivery, the pick of the litter is UPS, followed closely by DHL; both are quite reliable and have functional tracking numbers. FedEx provides excellent service in the United States but to a great extent subcontracts deliveries in Latin America.

We have now worked our way through the various steps you must consider when making your initial contact in Latin America. This somewhat daunting task is made easier with this guidebook, which gives you the cultural background and takes you through the process one step at a time. Now that you have introduced yourself to your Latin American friends, it is time to consider the easiest and most efficient way to travel in Latin America.

# 2
# Traveling Smart

*Of all the unbearable nuisances, the ignoramus*
*that has travelled is the worst.*
—Kin Hubbard

Much time, energy and money can be wasted before you ever meet your prospective client. As a business traveler, you must learn the art of traveling quickly and efficiently, with sure knowledge and confidence in confronting the challenges that lie ahead. The idea that travel is a pleasure became obsolete decades ago, and lack of experience can definitely lead to problems in international travel. This chapter seeks to help you overcome some potential obstacles.

At the very latest, catch the first flight available on the day before your first business meeting. Do not schedule meetings on the day of your arrival. If your destination is at an altitude of more than six thousand feet, an even earlier arrival is suggested in order to acclimate your body to the thin air. You should also plan for an additional unscheduled day at the end of your stay for any rescheduled meetings and unforeseen opportunities that may arise during your trip.

# PASSPORTS

Make sure your passport has at least six months' validity before you begin your travels. Many countries won't accept a passport with less than that and will refuse you entry. With the recent change in U.S. passport regulations, obtaining a passport or a renewal is a slow process. Even if you pay all of the expediting fees, it can take weeks for you to receive your travel document.

It's a good practice also to carry on your person a document listing your name, your local address, a stateside contact person's name and telephone numbers, your blood type and any medical problems you might have. In addition, copy onto this document the identification page in your passport. This paper is important should you become incapacitated. It is generally best to leave the passport itself in the safe at the hotel. Losing it presents too much of an inconvenience.

# VISAS

Tourist visas or cards are usually no problem and can be obtained at the airport upon arrival. Exceptions are noted under the individual countries covered in Part Two. It is recommended that you use tourist visas—also known as entry permits—whenever feasible. You will then be passed through entry to most countries with minimal formalities. If you are planning any tourism during your stay, when asked your reason for travel, you can say it is for vacation. You'll get a one-entry tourist visa or card and be on your way. Emphasizing the tourist part of the trip is legal if you are going to do any sightseeing at all, and it is difficult to avoid being at least partially a tourist on any business trip. This is the easier way to travel and many business travelers utilize this type of visa. Keep careful track of your tourist visa or card because you must surrender it upon leaving the country or pay a substantial fine.

If upon arrival you say that your visit is for business purposes, you will be required to present a business visa. The business visa must be arranged with the appropriate national consulate, or consulates if you are traveling to multiple countries, before you leave the United States. Allow four to twelve weeks for this process, depending on the countries to be visited, although some travelers utilize commercial visa services found on the net and in the yellow pages, which claim to provide greater speed. If you can physically find a local service, it would provide an opportunity to visit their office with your questions and concerns. Check with the Better Business Bureau for any current complaints against these services, although this will probably require you to call the service first, as these companies customarily do not provide a physical address. Take a chance with them if you are pressed for time. You must satisfy all the various paperwork requirements, but once obtained, business visas are good for multiple reentries. The rules for business visas for each country vary. Check with the national consulate and in Part Two of this book before you leave.

There are only two situations in which you absolutely must possess a business visa:

- If you are carrying what are obviously samples of merchandise, you will need a business visa to clear the product through Latin American customs.

Samples will cause delays at the customs kiosk, so schedule for that. If you have a quantity of relatively high-value samples or are traveling from country to country, consider obtaining an ATA Carnet, a special document that will somewhat ease your way through customs.

- If your intent is to sign a contract while in that country, if the contract is ever challenged in court and it is found that you came in on a tourist visa, it can be alleged that you entered the country illegally and that the contract is therefore invalid.

## NEGOTIATING THE LATIN AMERICAN AIRPORT

The lines at Latin American immigration at your destination can be more than an hour's duration, through which you are standing in the heat and humidity, plus you still also have the wait to clear customs. Make sure you have a bottle of water with you when you leave the airplane, to combat the dehydration, as nothing potable is available once you enter the immigration area. If you don't have water of your own, beg a couple of bottles from the flight attendants. They will understand.

At a Latin American border, you may find it prudent to offer the customs officials a *refresco* (see page 57) to clear you through without harassment or delay. This is indicated when some unexpected or inexplicable difficulties present themselves and it becomes apparent to you that this tip is expected. Ordinary tourists entering Mexico by air are usually exempt, but don't be afraid to subtly offer a *refresco* if needed. Keep a few five-dollar bills loose in your pocket for this eventuality. Be businesslike and friendly but create an air of being in command. Do not assume the role of a victim. But leave the Rolex watch at home. You also don't want to appear to be a flashy and affluent gringo.

Leaving each country, there is an airport tax, which you pay over and above the price of your ticket. You must pay this in the local currency. Credit cards and dollars are usually not accepted, so save some local cash for this purpose.

## DEALING WITH LOST BAGGAGE

Lost or stolen bags, not an unusual occurrence in Latin America, present special challenges for the business traveler over and above the normal inconvenience experienced by a tourist. Of course, you know never to put your medicines or anything of value in a suitcase. Appropriate replacement clothes may be hard to find locally unless you wear smaller sizes. This is true for suits, shirts, undergarments, socks and shoes. In addition, you will need to allow time for alterations. You should not go into a meeting in your distressed and rumpled traveling clothes. Excuses sound trite and elicit pity rather than respect.

Spring into immediate action when your bags are not made available after your flight arrives. Start looking for a suit no matter what redress the airline promises. Always leave a free day at the beginning and end of your trip for such contingencies so you can put something together or reschedule if need be. If you can assemble just one outfit, most of the international hotels have overnight dry cleaning and laundry services. Do not delay in anticipation of the best from the airline. Your odds are not good.

If you lose your prescription medicine, just about everything that is a prescription drug in the United States is available over the counter in Latin America at substantially reduced prices. The larger pharmacies provide the same brands as in the United States. Drugs are not dispensed into open containers but rather are sold in fixed quantity and in sealed packets, with the sale price indicated on the package label by the supplier, along with an expiration date.

Some travelers stock up on prescription drugs. It is legal to bring back fifty doses of a particular medicine for personal use. The exception is the purchase of prescription drugs deemed to be painkillers, which require a local prescription. This document can usually be obtained from the pharmacy for a small fee, without the inconvenience of you actually seeing a doctor.

## THE TRIP TO YOUR HOTEL

Anticipate a long and slow taxi ride to get to your hotel. It will be well over an hour's duration if you are entering a major metropolitan area. Don't select your own taxi at the airport, as you won't know what you will be getting into, literally or figuratively. There are all sorts of problems associated with travelers picking up a gypsy or unlicensed taxicab, which may be an unreliable, unsafe vehicle and will likely be uninsured. Avoid these cabs and look for an official taxi stand or dispatcher at the airport. You will prepay for a taxi trip to your destination, which is usually cheaper than what you'd pay for an unlicensed cab.

If you ever must secure a taxi on the street, look for an "official" vehicle and negotiate the fare in advance. Check to see that the driver's license is in the window and that the photograph on the permit matches the driver's face. Try to sound confident and stay in command. If you see a meter in the taxi, make sure it is activated. If it is not, tell the driver to turn it on, which may not be his practice when transporting foreigners. If he refuses, get out of the cab immediately. Listen to your gut instinct in this matter, and if it tells you that something is not quite right, pass on that taxi and wait for another.

## Smart Travel Tips

1. If you happen to be on a bus, you will notice that as a matter of courtesy, people entering say "*Buenos días*" to everyone else on the bus as they pass along the aisle. If the bus is crowded, they will only greet one of the senior citizens sitting next to the driver. Note that the two seats opposite the driver may be vacant even in a crowded bus. Do not use them, even if it means you are required to stand, as they are unofficially reserved for very senior citizens.

2. If you ever must ask for directions on the street, be aware of a Latin American idiosyncrasy. The person you ask will know the general direction you should be going or will consult with another passerby to find out. You will be pointed in the right direction and told "*cuatro cuadras*," or four blocks. Like the Irish mile and the scriptural number forty, this distance

is not to be taken literally. When you do not arrive at your destination after having traversed the four blocks, and you make another inquiry, you are likely to be pointed again in the direction you are traveling and informed *"cuatro cuadras."* When you hear four blocks as part of your travel directions, consider a form of transportation other than walking.

---

## SELECTING A HOTEL LOCATION

You will be exhausted and behind schedule by the time you get to your hotel. Plan on it. This is one of the reasons why hotel location is an extremely important consideration. A taxi ride from your hotel across a large city in search of your client can literally take hours. This is an expense, delay and stress inducer that you don't need. It will take some research, but you must locate a hotel near your clients. Ask your clients for a local recommendation. They will be happy to make one and even be able to provide attractive "local" rates, which are traditionally offered to local businesses that operate in the vicinity. In addition, it gives your clients the opportunity to do something nice for you at little inconvenience to themselves, builds relationships and provides a conversational gambit when you arrive.

If you have multiple stops in a city, map them before you leave, to find a suitable central location. Your clients may well be located in far-flung and inaccessible *colonias*, or suburbs, far from the city center, where it can be difficult to secure a taxi for the return trip. Make the best decision you can to minimize taxi travel.

With location pinpointed, there is usually a variety of hotel choices. Many business travelers prefer the international hotel chains. Standards are more or less predictable and they have convenient facilities. Other more intrepid types prefer an American- or Canadian-operated B and B. Here you should find invaluable advice and recommendations from the North American proprietor, and it will feel like home, providing comfort food for the soul. These establishments are easily located on the Internet. Email ahead with any questions, thereby making your first local contact.

Female travelers might consider avoiding a hotel at which the room doors open onto an exterior hallway, which might be the situation outside of downtown urban areas. Such establishments generally lack the security inherent in a more closed environment.

## EFFECTS OF ALTITUDE

Many Latin American cities are located at an altitude of more than 6,000 feet, and you may experience physical difficulties because of this. La Paz in Bolivia is at an altitude of 13,500 feet. Carrying your luggage any distance there might leave you lying on the ground gasping for air no matter what kind of physical shape you think you're in. Symptoms of altitude sickness often manifest themselves within six to ten hours after arrival and generally subside after a few days. Problems include headache, fatigue, stomach problems, dizziness and sleep disturbance. Any exertion, such as walking, aggravates these symptoms. Be aware that at high altitude, alcohol is metabolized quickly and you can become drunk on very little. Also remember that food is digested slowly at high altitude, and a large American-style breakfast will still be with you into the afternoon. Take it easy.

People with other serious physical challenges may find that these are exacerbated by altitude, but there seems to be no relationship between altitude sickness and age, sex and weight. There is no medicine for the malady and the only cure is time and rest. If you are traveling to Mexico City, which is at 7,500 feet, it is prudent to have a full day to rest after arriving to acclimate your body. At this altitude there is about 20 percent less oxygen in the air than at ground level. At 9,000 feet, two days would be required, and at 13,500 feet, three days, for your body to manufacture additional red blood cells to carry the oxygen to your brain. Some of the better hotels in La Paz, Bolivia, provide an oxygen mask by your bedside so that you can get a decent night's sleep. This oxygen deprivation combined with the endemic pollution does bad things to your body. A brain deprived of oxygen is an impediment to success, but given the above advice and the assistance available, is no excuse for returning home without a contract.

## RELATIONS WITH THE POLICE

This is one of the major cultural differences between the United States and Latin America. Police in Latin America are not your friends, and many of the locals do not even report crime to the police, believing as they do that not only will the police do nothing, they are probably collaborating with the criminals. In many places in Latin America, our concept of "protection under the law" is a sort of joke.

There are several classifications of police on the local, state and national levels. They generally share the following characteristics:

- In most jurisdictions, only an elementary school diploma is required for police service, and even this minimal requirement is sometimes waived. There are no college-level criminal justice programs in Latin America.
- The wages are incredibly low, with some jurisdictions paying their officers the equivalent of $25 to $30 a week. It is virtually impossible for a police officer to raise a family on this wage. Waitstaff in tourist restaurants or taxi drivers make much more. Hence the frequent necessity to solicit *refrescos*—or small bribes—in order to survive.
- Stability, due in part to the low wages, is an issue. Many departments experience an annual turnover approaching 100 percent.

If detained by the police, you are considered guilty until you can prove to the police that you are innocent. This is a characteristic of the Napoleonic Code of Law, which governs in Latin America. You may go to jail and spend days, weeks and even months before you are officially charged with anything. A very well-connected lawyer may or may not be able to expedite the process a bit.

Under Latin American criminal law, there is no bail or habeas corpus as there is in our English-based common law. You have zero rights. No right to a telephone call to notify family of your situation, no right to a trial by jury, no right to confront your accuser and no right to a speedy trial. In some countries, you must pay for your room and board while in prison. Prison conditions are worse than anything you can imagine, and this is particularly true for women. For example, in Bolivia, if you want something more than a very small cage, it can cost bribes of up to $5,000 a week. In some smaller countries you could say that throwing you in jail is a type of cottage industry.

There are literally tens of thousands of references to Latin American police corruption on the Internet and in literature, but quantification for comparison to the United States is impossible. The U.S. government does not keep such statistics, at least for publication, and the nations involved are loath to release any information they do have. A review of the literature suggests that the Latin American leaders in police corruption are Colombia, Brazil, Venezuela and El Salvador.

Based on the chart given below, we can see that Central and South America are dangerous places, which have murder rates at least three times higher than that of the United States.

## Murder Rates by Region

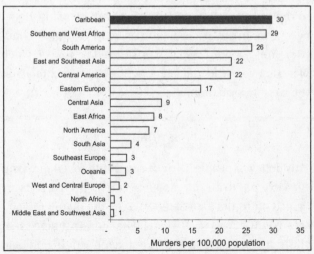

| Region | Murders per 100,000 population |
| --- | --- |
| Caribbean | 30 |
| Southern and West Africa | 29 |
| South America | 26 |
| East and Southeast Asia | 22 |
| Central America | 22 |
| Eastern Europe | 17 |
| Central Asia | 9 |
| East Africa | 8 |
| North America | 7 |
| South Asia | 4 |
| Southeast Europe | 3 |
| Oceania | 3 |
| West and Central Europe | 2 |
| North Africa | 1 |
| Middle East and Southwest Asia | 1 |

Murders per 100,000 population

**Source:** UNODC Crime Trends Surveys and Interpol, 2002 or most recent year.

If you are detained for any reason, bogus or not, it is definitely in your interest to stay calm and settle the matter privately with the police officer(s) who arrested you. The police are well aware that this is the normal expectation on all sides. It profits neither the officer nor his superiors personally if he hauls you off to jail, so settle with the police even if you are innocent and can prove it. It's cheaper and easier than any conceivable alternative. Negotiate! Remember that there are no juries in Latin American trials, and if it ever reaches that point it will be a foreigner's word against the local police.

If you are detained and unable to settle the matter immediately with the police, your next step is to contact the nearest American consulate whenever you can. They will recommend a lawyer and usually send a representative to visit you. Some countries, including Venezuela and Bolivia, have ejected our ambassador for political reasons related to supposed American imperialism, and so this recourse there would be problematic. This should be a factor in any decision you make to visit these countries. You should check *The CIA World Factbook* when planning your trip and again before departure, to assess the latest information.

## DRIVING

This policy of people being guilty until proven innocent even extends to an automobile accident. Both drivers are hauled off to the police station until the matter of damages is settled between them. The auto insurance that you must buy, if you are intent upon driving, should cover uninsured drivers (the majority) and have a provision that in the event of an accident the insurance company will more or less immediately dispatch a lawyer to the police station and settle matters on the spot or post a bond to secure your release. This is also the reason there are so many hit-and-run accidents in Latin America. The drivers do not want to go through the hassle of a trip to the police station. The bottom line is: try not to drive in Latin America. Secure the services of a driver and let the driver handle the situation in the event of a fender bender.

U.S. auto insurance is not valid in Latin America. You must secure a local insurance policy, which is sold by the day, week or month. If you're driving across the Mexican border, there are numerous well-advertised kiosks at the border where such insurance can be purchased. Sanborn's is one of the largest and most reliable providers. If you are renting a car, the insurance comes with the rental fee. Make sure the policy covers both uninsured drivers and legal assistance. Claims that your U.S. auto insurance will cover you wherever you go fall on deaf ears.

## Warning About Demonstrations

If you ever come upon a demonstration, strike or any other type of loud crowd activity in Latin America, go the other way immediately. Your natural instinct may be, as mine is, to stand there to witness what occurs, and you may even be drawn toward the commotion. Do not go there! Many curious foreigners are caught up in these demonstrations, which turn violent with amazing rapidity and regularity. Tear gas gets into your clothing and it is very difficult for dry cleaners to remove the smell. I was observing one such commotion, and when it turned nasty, I ducked into a restaurant. A police officer threw a tear gas canister in after me, and in the noxious fumes, I could not find the rear exit. No fun at all!

It is hard to turn on your television in Latin America without witnessing such demonstrations, even in such otherwise stable countries as Chile. Unlike in the United States, where relatively gentle methods of crowd control are customary, the liberal use of gas, water cannons and batons by the police or paramilitary (the equivalent of our National Guard) is very common in such demonstrations. If you are part of the crowd, you are a potential target. There are no civil rights and there is no judicial redress in the case of injury.

---

## HEALTH SERVICES AND INSURANCE

Health care in Latin America is problematic, except possibly in Mexico City, Buenos Aires and Rio de Janeiro, where you're likely to find privately run foreign hospitals, which may or may not meet minimum U.S. standards. Why such a problem?

First, there is no facile U.S.-style malpractice litigation under civil law in Latin America, so unreliable doctors can continue practicing until retirement, unencumbered by litigation. Second, there is no form of medical quality control, like the American Medical Association in the United States. Finally, you can trust health care to be unreliable in government-run hospitals, which are traditionally grossly underfunded. In these institutions, families are expected to attend to the physical needs of the patient on a twenty-four-hour basis and to provide the meals.

If you become ill, if possible, head for home immediately. If this is not possible, call, or have an associate call, the nearest American consulate for a medical recommendation. A consular official will visit you at the hospital to coordinate assistance.

Your stateside health insurance won't be accepted in Latin American hospitals, so you should make provisions for medical payment in case you need hospitalization. Credit cards are usually accepted. I became seriously ill in Mexico City and headed for the American British Cowdray (ABC) Hospital because it was one of the most reputable in the city and the Blue Cross website indicated it was the only local hospital in the city that accepted my insurance. I'd let my evacuation insurance lapse. This insurance, which pays for medical evacuation by air in the event of an emergency, is recommended if you are going to spend much time in Latin America. As it turned out, the hospital had not accepted Blue Cross for several years and required a $10,000 deposit prior to admission. The most viable solution for me was to be assisted by my good Mexican friends to the airport, where the first available flight took me to Texas and the Houston Medical Center. In such circumstances, whether incapacitated by illness, accident or criminal activity, it is helpful to have an administrative assistant as discussed in Chapter 3. This person can contact your home office, your family and even the consulate. Without friends, an assistant or insurance, you are a stranger in a foreign land and dependent upon the kindness of strangers, which is not always forthcoming.

If contacted in such matters, the local consulate should direct you to a local hospital or even call an air ambulance, but you must absorb the cost, which can be up to $20,000 or more depending on the distances involved, and such expenses are not reimbursable by standard health insurance. When you are very sick and feeling vulnerable, this can be an especially disquieting experience.

Keep copies of your medical invoices. Most U.S. insurance companies will, after the requisite mountain of paperwork, reimburse you for your medical expenses. It is best to check with your medical insurer for your coverage in these situations.

There are several companies that provide international health insurance that includes evacuation expenses. If you intend to be in Latin America for any length of time, international health insurance is strongly recommended. Three of many possibilities can be found at www.health careinternational.com, www.travelhealthinsurance.com and www.international-medical-insurance.com.

We have seen in this chapter that traveling smart is a requirement if you wish to be successful. There are obstacles and even dangers that you can encounter, over which you have no control and which require an appropriate response if you are to successfully move forward. This chapter covered the most common problems, but if you are faced with an unanticipated challenge, consider it to be a learning experience. Stay cool!

# 3
# Getting Help with Your Communications

*Only he who has traveled knows*
*where the holes are deep.*
—Chinese proverb

Traveling alone, and without a support system to help with your communications and other transactions, is not the most productive way to conduct business. If you don't work for a company that supplies such services, it is up to you to look to your own devices and create a support system for yourself. Fortunately, securing these services is not an overwhelming task, if you know what to do and how to do it. That is the focus of this chapter.

Hiring a few key hourly people will help you make the most efficient use of your time. The costs for doing this in Latin America are very low compared to those in the United States. There will be inevitable roadblocks when doing business in a new culture, and you should not try to conquer them alone. The following types of assistance are recommended.

## BILINGUAL ADMINISTRATIVE ASSISTANT

An administrative assistant, or "admin," is the person who will help you with all aspects of communication. This person is nearly indispensable for an effective, stress-free business experience in Latin America if your Spanish is not adequate for your business needs. Going it alone is, of course, possible, but not to be recommended. Among the duties of an administrative assistant are reconfirming appointments, giving directions and paying the taxi, finding the right office, introducing you to your clients, doing minor translating, and providing you with the general real-time minute-by-minute support, advice, and local assistance necessary to make your trip as effective and as pleasant as possible. In addition to these obvious benefits, there are also a number of more subtle effects.

When you walk into a meeting, having someone to figuratively "carry your briefcase" gives you a gravitas you would not enjoy if you were flying solo. Important people have an entourage. Even more so than in the United States, in Latin America you are judged on how you present yourself, because to a certain extent appearances seem to equal reality there.

In the event of a physical problem or an accident, having someone along to help deal with the consequences is of unquestionable value.

After the initial trip, some minor administrative follow-up may be required with your prospective client prior to your next visit. Your local Latin America–based administrative assistant is aware of the local situation and can be entrusted with this type of work. You can effectively use email when corresponding with your admin, as the person contacted is your contractual employee.

## Cost Efficiency of Administrative Assistants

Carefully consider what your business trip is actually costing you. The cost of your time during your Latin American trip has a value greater than your salary plus benefits. There is the monetary cost of the trip itself, including airfare, hotel, food, entertainment, local transportation and incidentals. To determine the actual cost of each contact hour with your clients, add up the total cost of the following:

Your daily salary plus benefits for the period you will be traveling

International transportation costs

Hotels

Food

Local transportation costs in Latin America

Entertainment

Incidental costs

Total the above and multiply it by the number of days you are traveling. Average the total for each day. Subtract your hours of daily downtime from twelve, which is your average number of hours of available work time per day. The result will equal your hours of contact time. Divide the total cost of the trip by your total hours of contact time.

This will provide the dollar amount for each hour you

have available to spend with a client. The cost per hour may prove startling. Don't count sleep or any downtime as part of your contact hours. Downtime is defined as any time you are not directly interacting with your client and includes local travel, delayed meetings, getting lost or just hanging around waiting. Eliminating downtime is impossible, but you can strive to minimize it, and as you minimize downtime, the cost of each available contact hour also goes down. Each hour eliminated from downtime gives you an additional hour with your client at no additional cost to you.

Your actual cost per available working contact hour will likely exceed $200 and perhaps be a great deal higher, depending on how you schedule your time. Therefore, waste as little of the available work time as possible. Since travel and sleep time are relatively fixed, the only thing you can control to a certain extent is your downtime.

When an actual cost of well over $200 per working hour is paid by you or your company, it is economically prudent to secure an assistant to help you make efficient use of your valuable time. The cost is modest. For highly qualified people, expect to spend $15 per hour in the large metropolitan areas and less in the smaller cities. As an additional benefit, with this type of help, you will be more relaxed and better able to effectively concentrate on your business—which is the purpose of your trip—while the administrative assistant smooths the path for you.

### Finding an Administrative Assistant

Locating an appropriate individual is not difficult. Start at home by checking for recommendations from your business associates who have traveled to Latin America in the past. You can ask around for someone in your organization who has a friend or relative at your destination who can be brought into service. A call from your office to the university placement office in that area is an excellent option. It will certainly produce a good part-time business student, although if you don't speak Spanish, it might be necessary to have a Spanish speaker initiate the call to negotiate the university bureaucracy. It would be optimal to speak with your potential administrative assistant prior to arriving in Latin America. This call could be used to clarify any questions remaining for you and to confirm your arrangements with that person. Be sure the question of compensation is discussed. If all this fails, prior to departure you can also check the local American consulate, which keeps a directory of available individuals, and ask them for a recommendation. The concierge at your hotel may also be helpful, but concierge recommendations tend to be for formal translators, which is not what you need.

The person you are looking for must be a professionally dressed local resident with strong English skills. The hours are determined by your particular needs, although I suggest starting your assistant's shift at breakfast and keeping the admin on the clock until after the last business meeting of the day. If the administrative assistant seems sociable and an evening's entertainment is scheduled where you believe that there will be non-English speakers present, you might consider inviting and paying the admin to do minor translating at that function. Some business travelers have an admin waiting for them at the airport when they arrive and have a planning session on the way back to the hotel. All of this assistance is a modest investment considering the tremendous cost/benefit ratio.

## DEDICATED DRIVER

In addition to an administrative assistant, one of the expense items to be considered when estimating your budget for the trip should be a chauffeur. Some companies provide this support as a matter of policy, while others leave it to the devices of the traveling executive. If necessary, clear this expense item with your CFO before leaving, and if there's resistance, be sure to point out that a driver hired on an hourly or daily basis is actually economical. Your time, energy and well-being are valuable. Consider your cost per hour on the ground. The driver will get you quickly and safely from place to place, dropping you off in front of the right door. The cost is not much higher than taking a series of taxicabs. In some industrial neighborhoods in which your clients may be located, taxis can be hard to find after a meeting. In addition, when you climb into a street taxi, you are taking an unnecessary risk. Your personal driver will literally (they usually keep a few bottles of water in the car) and figuratively carry water for you.

Reliable drivers are easy to find, usually attached to hotels and sometimes referred to as "hotel cars." If you are going to be making repeat visits to a particular city, you will, in time, select your favorite driver at your favorite hotel and become friends. In Mexico City, I usually stay at the Stella Maris, a small business hotel, and Sr. Toledo is my driver. I know this driver and his children, and occasionally we all go out to lunch together. It is the Latin American way.

In case you should ever be required to actually operate an automobile in an emergency, it is a good idea to carry an international driver's license. Contingencies should be covered as far as possible and this one is easy to cover. The license is inexpensive and easy to obtain through the AAA.

## TRANSLATOR

Hiring a translator requires some careful consideration. In general, the farther south into Latin America you go and the farther from a major metropolitan area you travel, the more likely you are to need a translator. That being said, there are some additional considerations. Latin Americans are justifiably proud of their hard-earned knowledge of English. Determine if your client speaks even minimal English. If he does, is it sufficient to conduct business? Many times you will find that the answer to the first question is yes and the second is no.

If your client speaks adequate English or you speak adequate Spanish, then you do not need a translator. Few things are more awkward than to show up with a translator and find that your client has graduated from Harvard and just finished a five-year stint in the United States.

The most difficulty can arise when you introduce a translator into a situation where your client really believes his English to be sufficient. This is a delicate situation and you should not give offense. If you sense this is developing, an explanation along the lines of "Your

English is excellent, Sr. Gómez, and my Spanish is very poor. We are talking about complicated issues, and I just want to be certain that we each understand exactly what the other means, and therefore I have brought a translator so there is never any confusion" may help alleviate his concern.

Unless your Spanish is excellent enough that you can conduct business in Spanish, attempt before you leave to consult with someone who knows the prospective client, or get your client on the telephone from the United States and make the best assessment possible. Sometimes this evaluation is tricky. Listen for vocabulary, because many executives have a very facile command of a very limited vocabulary, which can fool you and which falls apart during negotiations. You may believe everything is going along swimmingly in English and be unaware that your client understands about a third of what you are saying and what you think he is agreeing to.

It can also be taken as an insult if you introduce a translator at a second meeting, indicating that you think your client's English was insufficient at the first meeting. A difficult call in a delicate situation. If faced with this, do not try to introduce a translator as your friend or business associate, as this does not work. Be honest and say that you would prefer to communicate in Spanish because of the importance of what you are discussing and that errors in communication are not good when talking to a friend.

With an administrative assistant in tow, you can usually cover your communication needs for the first meeting. However, when it comes down to business contracts,

you should have a professional translator who understands the nuances of the language. It is very easy for
confusion and misunderstanding to creep into a bilingual conversation when money is involved.

Learn at least some Spanish. Many nouns are recog-
nizable to an English speaker. Numbers, directions and
courtesy phrases, along with restaurant-menu Spanish,
should be the minimum at your command. More is better, and any effort on your part will be appreciated by
your Latin American client. Get a Spanish-language
training CD. It can be fun. If nothing else, learn the
common business terms contained in the appendix.

Professional translators are easy to find. The American consulate keeps a directory, as will the concierge at
most hotels. Translators charge by the hour, and by the
page for translating documents. Be sure to negotiate a
rate before you employ the person.

## BANKER

If you spend substantial time in Latin America or conduct business there beyond the simplest sales calls, you
will inevitably become involved with a bank. This can
be a frustrating experience for you because it will be
necessary for you to appear personally to perform routine functions. Everything in Latin American banking is
essentially built on personal identification, which at this
point in the book should be of no surprise to you.

A great deal of information is required by the government for transactions such as opening an account,
whether it's personal or business. To open a business

account, a stack of government documents and personal data is required, but it goes far beyond this and deeper into the Latin American character. A normal visit with your banker, involving something simple, such as a deposit, a withdrawal, a certified check or a change in an existing account, which you could accomplish at an ATM or online in the United States, can take three valuable hours of your time in Latin America. It sounds incredible, and it is difficult to reconstruct how the time slips away in waiting for an officer, paperwork shuffling and seemingly random conversations, but it is the Latin American way. No one is in a hurry and what is not accomplished today can be done tomorrow. The bankers are curious about Americans and want to learn everything possible about you and your situation beyond your current banking requirements. This takes time, but take advantage of this characteristic by converting this downtime into productive time. Use these hours wisely by gathering information and insinuating yourself into the banker's affinity circle. Relax and do not waste time and energy swimming against the tide. Rather, let the flow carry you to your destination, which is success.

Socialize first and build a relationship. Get to know a friendly bank officer who speaks English. Make a *comida* date and you will be richly rewarded, as bankers are a fountain of useful information. If no friendly English-speaking officer is available, go to another branch or bank.

Ask your home bank if they have a relationship with an institution at your destination and try that bank first, as this contact may ease your way. Remember to secure a letter of introduction from your bank and present it at the first meeting.

Banks are usually open only in the mornings. They do not reopen after the *comida* break.

## LAWYER

If you are making anything more complex than a sales call, you will need an English-speaking lawyer because a local attorney should review any document that you are required to sign. Do not use your lawyer in the United States. Contracts in Latin America are written based on civil law and not the common law we use here, and terms have different meanings.

Selection of a lawyer in Latin America is about as simple as finding a reputable lawyer in the United States. The U.S. consulate maintains a list of lawyers who they believe are honest, but, of course, their performance cannot be guaranteed. If you have Latin American friends who are not commercially connected to the contract, you might ask them for recommendations. You can also check the various Latin American legal associations, which maintain lists of their membership on the Internet. You may view a list of these associations by country at www.hg.org/latinam-bar. It is always prudent to check several references.

When hiring someone as your employee, instead of as an independent contractor, you will need a lawyer. It is easy to hire and very difficult and expensive to fire an employee in Latin America.

If you buy a business with employees in situ, make sure all accrued benefits have been paid to them before purchase and that you have no future obligations to them. Essentially you want the old ownership to dismiss everyone and pay the fees, and you then hire the people you want and start all over. To avoid paying these fees, some employers keep incompetents on the payroll and stick a new owner with the cost of firing them.

In many situations, you must go into the local labor courts to prove legally your reasons for firing even an employee who is a thief, incompetent and a drunk to boot. And this will not necessarily be an easy task. As a North American, don't expect automatically to have a satisfactory outcome in local courts even if your cause is just. Some people want to be hired just so that they can be fired and sue you.

It is vitally important for you to secure competent legal advice before you begin to negotiate the purchase of a company or the establishment of a distributorship. The laws concerning these matters differ substantially from country to country and can in the minds of some North Americans seem quite peculiar.

In this chapter we have demonstrated that you are not alone in your venture into Latin America. There is professional assistance available covering every aspect of your business life. Not to make use of this is foolhardy and makes a task that is complicated in and of itself even more so. Now that you have the help you need, we turn to one of the more challenging practices you will find—corruption.

# 4
# Corruption in Latin America

*Travel teaches toleration.*
—Benjamin Disraeli

In the minds of at least some North Americans, corruption is one of the distinguishing characteristics of the Latin American culture. Utilizing the classic definition of the term, this impression is valid, but in Latin America the word has a variant meaning. It involves an easygoing "You scratch my back and I'll scratch yours" type of mentality, and this corruption is widely tolerated by all. A case could be made for the proposition that this pervasive Latin American variant on corruption is the foundation of the economy. In a society where efficient performance is not necessarily valued, the remuneration gathered through this mechanism can sometimes be seen to replace the just compensation that might be earned in other cultures. Quid pro quo is the order of the day! Individuals who insist on adherence to the letter of the law will be in for some rough sledding.

## BUREAUCRATIC INTERFACE OR AGENT

This functionary is sometimes identified as a *gator*, consultant, trading company or attorney. The position, which goes by so many different titles, may be unfamiliar to you, unless you have dealt with a particularly venal lobbyist. If you spend any time or do substantial business in Latin America, you are going to need the services of this type of provider. The size and complexity of the Latin American bureaucracy can be truly astounding to many North Americans. Even the simplest function requires copious slow-moving paperwork. The extension of a visa, the opening of a bank account, obtaining an export permit, registering an automobile, renting an office space, opening a business, hiring someone, firing someone, getting a cell phone or a land line, and virtually any other activity requires more time and effort than you would ever dream of.

The bureaucrat that controls these processes is likely a political appointee or—since nepotism is common—a relative of his superior who has minimal interest in his job. The well-being of his organization is not a consideration. There is nothing you can do about it. Complaints are met with a smile. They make the rules and you are the guest in their country. The system has been characterized by many individuals and organizations such as Amnesty International as institutionalized or endemic corruption, which is a novel concept for us in the United States and is one of the major problems with doing business in Latin America.

When and if the time eventually comes to offer a solicited incentive to a local bureaucrat, your admin might be able to suggest an appropriate amount. Your agent, who has been employed to handle such matters and who will actually present the payment, may unbeknownst to you not actually present the entire bribe and retain a part of the payment for himself. It would be an understatement to say that the honesty of such functionaries cannot be taken for granted.

## Dealing with Corruption in Latin America

Latin America's corrupt bureaucracy is perhaps best summarized by the *Corruptions Perceptions Index*, an annual report produced by Transparency International that ranks Latin American countries from the least corrupt (most recently Chile) to the most corrupt (most recently Paraguay), with Mexico currently occupying the exact center of the continuum.

## Corruption Perception Index (CPI) for Latin America (Transparency International)
### (0 = most corrupt; 10 = least corrupt)

|  | 1995 | 1996 | 1997 | 1998 | 1999 | 2000 | 2001 | 2002 | 2003 | Avg. | Rank |
|---|---|---|---|---|---|---|---|---|---|---|---|
| Argentina | 5.24 | 3.41 | 2.81 | 3.0 | 3.1 | 3.5 | 3.5 | 2.8 | 2.5 | 3.34 | 10 |
| Bolivia |  | 3.40 | 2.05 | 2.8 | 2.5 | 2.7 | 2.0 | 2.2 | 2.3 | 2.49 | 17 |
| Brazil | 2.70 | 2.96 | 3.56 | 4.0 | 4.1 | 3.9 | 4.0 | 4.0 | 3.9 | 3.69 | 8 |
| Chile | 7.94 | 6.80 | 6.05 | 6.8 | 6.9 | 7.4 | 7.5 | 7.5 | 7.4 | 7.13 | 1 |
| Colombia | 3.44 | 2.73 | 2.23 | 2.2 | 2.9 | 3.2 | 3.8 | 3.6 | 3.7 | 3.08 | 13 |
| Costa Rica |  |  |  | 5.6 | 5.1 | 5.4 | 4.5 | 4.5 | 4.3 | 4.90 | 2 |
| Cuba |  |  |  |  |  |  |  |  | 4.6 | 4.60 | 4 |
| Dominican Republic |  |  |  |  |  |  | 3.1 | 3.5 | 3.3 | 3.30 | 12 |
| Ecuador |  | 3.19 |  | 2.3 | 2.4 | 2.6 | 2.3 | 2.2 | 2.2 | 2.46 | 18 |
| El Salvador |  |  |  | 3.6 | 3.9 | 4.1 | 3.6 | 3.4 | 3.7 | 3.72 | 7 |
| Guatemala |  |  |  | 3.1 | 3.2 | 2.9 | 2.5 |  | 2.4 | 2.82 | 14 |
| Haiti |  |  |  |  |  |  |  | 2.2 | 1.5 | 1.85 | 20 |
| Honduras |  |  |  | 1.7 | 1.8 |  | 2.7 | 2.7 | 2.3 | 2.24 | 19 |
| Jamaica |  |  |  |  |  |  |  |  | 3.8 | 3.80 | 6 |
| Mexico | 3.18 | 3.30 | 2.66 | 3.3 | 3.4 | 3.3 | 3.7 | 3.6 | 3.6 | 3.34 | 10 |
| Nicaragua |  |  |  |  | 3.1 |  | 2.4 | 2.5 | 2.6 | 2.65 | 15 |
| Panama |  |  |  |  |  |  | 3.7 | 3.0 | 3.4 | 3.37 | 9 |
| Paraguay |  |  |  | 1.5 | 2.0 |  |  | 1.7 | 1.6 | 1.70 | 21 |
| Peru |  |  |  | 4.5 |  | 4.4 | 4.1 | 4.0 | 3.7 | 4.14 | 5 |
| Uruguay |  |  | 4.14 | 4.3 |  |  |  | 5.1 | 5.5 | 4.75 | 3 |
| Venezuela | 2.66 | 2.50 | 2.77 | 2.3 |  | 2.7 | 2.8 | 2.5 | 2.4 | 2.59 | 16 |

Although there is copious anecdotal material, statistical reporting in this area is difficult because individuals involved are loath to fill out surveys, and furthermore, the exact definition of "corruption" remains technically difficult. But some hard data has surfaced in recent years. One of the most detailed reports is an exhaustive document prepared by the United Nations Development Program (UNDP) entitled *Corruption and Governance Measurement Tools in Latin American Countries*, which provides dozens of links describing the local situations in detail. The full report can be accessed on the UNDP's website, www.undp.org.

For this reason, foreigners and most locals hire someone to interface with the various bureaucracies. The individuals who perform this function are usually retired mid-level bureaucrats themselves or old-time lawyers who "know everybody" and function like North American lobbyists. These independent agents are easy to find. The best source may be the individuals whom you know and who have done business in the area you're working in. Use the man they use to expedite formalities. Do not be shy about asking. Having someone available to serve in this capacity for you is normal business practice! The exact idiomatic title for the individual you are seeking varies from country to country, and most are vulgar, so they cannot be repeated here. *Gator* is used in Mexico and "consultant" is always a safe bet.

Your administrative assistant or translator should also be aware of individuals to recommend, as qualified people are not uncommon. I have used a lawyer whom I know and almost trust. However, make sure you make financial arrangements with this person before you begin. You could also ask the American consulate for their list of commercial agents. In every case, ask the proposed agent for a list of his satisfied clients, which he will be more than willing to provide. It is very difficult to avoid being overcharged. You are trusting a marginal person working without supervision, and they tend not to discriminate among clients. The topic of bribes is discussed in greater detail under *"Mordidas"* later in the chapter.

Consider the following all-too-common scenario. A permit is needed to open a distributorship for your company. Proper forms must be completed in all their intricacy, with multiple copies. This is usually done by a professional scribe, or *escritor*, who has all the complex forms and knows exactly what is required in each box. The services of this person are usually secured by your agent, who will unbeknownst to you add an unofficial commission to the fee. Next, your agent submits the mountain of forms to the proper agencies along with an official fee. The agent then informs you that the processing time for this paperwork is at least sixty days and perhaps much, much longer. This is both an accurate assessment of the situation by your agent and a very common scenario. However, he has a friend, cousin, coworker or mother who works in that particular office and can put the permit on top of the pile if she pays her boss $1,000. Naturally, the agent skims a percentage out of this "fee" in addition to what he is charging you directly for his services. You will never be sure whether he actually gave his confederate the $1,000 or just $200, pocketing the difference for his trouble.

It may be challenging to accept this as the normal

way to do business, because it runs so contrary to typical U.S. business traditions. Consult your administrative assistant to try to determine if any payment is reasonable. Since such open-ended delays are brutal to both your business and sanity, you'll be likely to concur and pay. The signed paperwork will be efficiently returned to you the next day.

It is technically illegal for government employees in Latin American to accept payment to perform their duties, but the practice is commonplace. It is illegal under U.S. law for payment to be made, but there is no public law in Latin America against private corruption in the corporate world. Hence the widely used practice of hiring local consultants to interface with the bureaucracy.

A major setback for North Americans who lack cultural understanding of Latin America is being fully aware that they are being ripped off and becoming angry. Get over it or get out! There is nothing you can do about it except pay these bribes. It is best to consider them just another cost of doing business in Latin America. You are the visitor and your host makes the rules. On the bright side, your official paperwork is expeditiously processed and you can get on with your life. You are spared the misery of dealing with these unpleasant bureaucrats on a face-to-face basis.

Under the U.S Foreign Corrupt Practices Act, it is illegal for an American to give bribes, payoffs, kickbacks or other favors in exchange for favored treatment. The same isn't true for citizens from other countries. This puts Americans executives at a severe competitive disadvantage in Latin America, where such payments are the norm. I would never advise anyone to carry out a criminal act. It is illegal under U.S. law to pay anyone a bribe, and you should not participate in the practice. This is the strongest recommendation I can make. Walk away if you must! However, it is legal to employ an independent agent or consultant to perform a task—e.g., secure a permit. You are paying the agent a lump sum and paying nothing to any official. What the consultant does with the money you pay him is technically none of your concern. There is no requirement that you make inquiry.

### PROPINAS, REFRESCOS AND MORDIDAS

Endemic institutionalized corruption can be found throughout Latin America. Bribes, large and small, grease the mechanisms and make the society function more smoothly, so you should not appear shocked or surprised by such practices when you encounter them. These are normal business and personal practices in Latin America. You will encounter several forms of bribery, each with its unique connotation. Various names are assigned to approximate dollar values. From the smallest amount to the largest they are:

• *Propinas.* In one sense, one of these is literally a tip, similar to what is offered in restaurants in the United States as an indication of gratitude after services have been rendered. Latin American waiters generally expect 15 percent. Other service providers should be tipped as they are in the United States.

However, *propinas* have other and much wider uses in Latin America. The *propina* is expected prior to or as a condition of rendering some services. The intent is to ensure that the services are rendered. An unofficial curbside parking attendant who waves his red bandana, guides you into a parking place on "his" public street, and watches your car expects a *propina*, as do the unofficial guards in supermarket parking lots. The fellow who fills up your car at the gas station expects a *propina*. The man who collects the garbage expects a bit each week. A dollar is more than enough for most of these services. Not to pay will offend the recipient and indicate that you are culturally insensitive.

It is generally considered boorish for a foreigner to walk by an obviously needy person on the sidewalk without dropping a coin into the basket. Expect to be prayed for or blessed in return for this payment, which is not such a bad thing. The same is not true for loud and aggressive street kids who go about begging. It is really a form of street extortion. Don't give these kids anything. They will increase the hassling, even if you do hand over some cash, and will draw a large crowd of their peers as you walk along. Ignore them, and after a short time they will select a more promising victim.

Small-scale scams like this are of seemingly infinite variety in Latin America. One evening an amiable shoeshine man approached me and I accepted his services. To my fault, I didn't ask the price. After completing the shine, he demanded $20 due to the special polish he'd used. I handed him $1, which is the normal price for such services. He started screaming at me and within seconds was joined by two of his shoeshine confederates who'd been lurking in the dark, as they appeared to operate as a pack. They were all bellowing and collecting a crowd. What to do? I started very loudly calling (an understatement) for police. An officer soon strode up to quell the disturbance, and the shoeshine men dissipated into the crowd. The police officer then requested to examine my documentation to check if I was in the country legally. I smiled, thanked him and placed $5 in his hand. He then offered to escort me safely to my hotel.

Such petty larceny is almost laughable, considering the picayune amounts involved. It becomes an issue only when we consider the offense some sort of personal affront to our dignity. In Latin America, you will be confronted by such situations. Smile, stay cool and enjoy the experience.

Interestingly, taxi drivers are normally not tipped except by foreigners who think the practice universal. I usually round up the fare to the nearest bill I have in my pocket, but the locals get their change back. This is up to you, but unlike in the other situations outlined here, you will not be expected to give a *propina* to taxi drivers.

• *Refrescos*. This literally translates to "sodas" or "soft drinks." A *refresco* is in the low $5 to $20 range of bribes. The concept is that the receiver should go and have a soda on you. Mountains have been moved with *refrescos*. You want your suit cleaned and pressed in an hour? Offer a *refresco*. A police officer is about to give you a ticket for some infraction? *Refresco*. Impossible reservations at a restaurant or a completely sold-out theater? *Refresco*. In short, whenever you are told something is impossible or you need something done, hold out $10 or $20 and it will generally be done—expeditiously. It is the way the business of Latin American society is conducted.

Remember, however, that you should never offer anything tacky to your client, as such a small gift would be considered an insult to your associate in a business setting if the obvious intent was to secure favorable treatment in some way. If a serious bribe is required, it will be made known to you during the course of your business relationship. *Refrescos* are the lubricant that makes the Latin American world turn. Outside of your business relationship, your Latin American client is dispensing *refrescos* at about the same rate you are, except it is not bothering him.

Don't be too judgmental in these matters. A police officer stops you after you make an illegal turn. You are in the wrong. He is a family man who hasn't been paid in weeks, not an unusual occurrence in Latin America. You would technically owe a fine, but here you pay the police officer directly so that he can feed his family. Such a situation may technically be unethical but it is the modus operandi in Latin America.

• **Mordidas.** This is a true classic bribe, and though its name means "bites," it involves substantial sums. When requested by your client, it usually represents 2 or 3 percent of the contract price as a kickback to the authorizing person, and this can be a very substantial sum. The practice is all too common. It is perfectly normal for your competitors from outside the United States to pay the bribe. Resisting the *mordida*, although you might feel smug in occupying the moral high ground, puts you at a serious competitive disadvantage because the cost of the *mordida* is often worked into the contract price. If you do not pay, you will not get the contract.

What to do if the suggestion of a *mordida* is made? If you don't pay, you most likely won't get the contract. When and if the bribe is suggested, it will be apparent that the important consideration for your client and perhaps his boss concerning this contract is how they can personally profit from the transaction. Lowest price is not the prime consideration, and the best interests of their organization are not part of the calculus. With the dismal levels of corporate compensation this scam might be the only way mid-level managers can augment their salary. However, this practice is not conducive to the long-term financial health of an organization, but then again Latin Americans live to a great extent in the present rather than the future.

During negotiations, there may be a friendly, very low-key suggestion concerning the *mordida*, with much smiling between amigos, although the term itself will probably never be mentioned. Perhaps it will happen in the course of a boozy *comida*, which is yet another reason for you to be wary of the alcohol. It is silly to negotiate, because the amount paid will have no bearing whatsoever on what you will eventually realize from the transaction. If the amount is 3 percent, then that amount is added to your bid. The cost is really being absorbed by your client's company because they are paying an amount higher than your bid. There is really nothing to discuss because either you play the game or you don't. Of course, you understand that your client does not personally get to keep all of the payment, but that portions must be distributed to his superiors up the corporate ladder.

If you do decide to go with the contract, always use a local agent (see page 49) to negotiate the final phases of a deal. You pay the agent his consulting fee and he passes most of it on to the client. The payment itself takes many forms. There might be a requirement in the contract that you hire a particular consulting firm at an inflated price, who will do nothing during the course of the contract, or an all-expense-paid vacation to some exotic spot for the client and his family as a guest of your country might be suggested. There is a lot of creativity in this area.

As you can see, the *mordida* does not always involve actual payment of cash, except in moderate-size transactions or with sales to the government in which cash payment is required. On larger transactions with private companies, the *mordida* will involve a kickback to the client of 2 or 3 percent of the contract value.

Most, if not all, large contracts require some sort of kickback. You can always say that this practice is dishonest and refuse to participate. Some do this. But if you do not participate, some other vendor who will "play ball" will get the contract. Your call!

## THE UNDERGROUND ECONOMY

*Do you want an invoice?* You may be asked this somewhat unusual question on any number of occasions, and it is best for you to know the real meaning of the question.

Do not be too quick to reply yes or no to this question because an invoice is not the same thing as a receipt, which your vendor will willingly supply. A receipt is a vendor-originated document that can easily be produced by your supplier, while an invoice is an officially numbered government document that becomes part of the company's tax records. The company issuing the invoice must add sales tax or value added tax (VAT) to the invoice balance.

The invoice rather than a receipt results in a sales tax payable by you to the government of at least 15 percent and perhaps much higher. If the vendor insists on providing a legal invoice with the VAT indicated, you must accept this invoice. If the option for invoice or receipt is offered to you, and you are not operating a Latin American business in which the VAT tax can be deducted from your corporate taxes, then, like better than 60 percent of buyers, you should decline the invoice and accept a receipt, thus avoiding the tax. This is the underground economy at work.

All Latin American countries possess an underground economy, with the notable exceptions of Chile and Uruguay, where the corrupt practice is not tolerated and not providing an invoice is a criminal offense. In these countries you must accept the invoice and pay your VAT tax. In Mexico, which is far from the worst offender in this respect, approximately 60 percent of the routine business activities are not reported to the government and no taxes are paid on this income. The person asking you if you want an invoice may well be in the majority who are active in the underground economy. For you not to pay the sales tax is not a criminal offense as it is in the United States.

This question won't be asked of you at a large business (e.g., a big grocery store, a gasoline station, a large restaurant chain), which has installed electronic record keeping and is easily subjected to audit by the taxing authorities, and therefore must pay the tax on all transactions. This is not true for local restaurants, local shops, and virtually all other smaller commercial environments, which are not registered with the government and which could not possibly supply an invoice for you if the document was requested. With these vendors, it is assumed that you do not want an invoice.

The receipt you will receive from your Latin American supplier will satisfy the record-keeping requirements of both your accountant and the IRS. For a casual purchase, there really is no good reason for you to demand an invoice. If someone tries to charge you a VAT tax and it is on a receipt and not a government invoice, object. He is cheating and pocketing your tax. You should refuse to pay the tax or you should demand an official invoice.

Thus ends our brief discussion of corruption in the Latin American environment. Now that you have a better grasp of the cultural mores concerning this issue, you can acclimate yourself, because cultural tolerance is an absolute requirement for acceptance in Latin America. You have been forced to face the conundrums associated with moral relativism—can what is wrong or immoral in North America be acceptable or moral in Latin America? My attitude has been to stay relaxed and, within limits, to go with the flow.

# 5
# Acclimating to
# the Culture

*Travel is glamorous only in retrospect.*
—Paul Theroux

By way of introduction we will see in this chapter that actually doing business in Latin America involves considerable preparation and perhaps some attitude adjustment on your part. It is not easy to fit into an alien culture. Strangers are generally not trusted, so you must make every effort to shed this status. Business in Latin America isn't conducted expeditiously, and it's not conducted at all until relationships are firmly established. We must be friends, not just North American executives. Business in Latin America is only conducted with individuals considered *simpático*. This term is defined in the dictionary as "nice," "likeable," "close" or "friendly," but there is perhaps no exact English counterpart. How to establish these culturally appropriate relationships through various forms of communication is the topic of this chapter.

Latin American business practices are built on relationships and not necessarily on price or credit availability, although the latter will eventually enter the picture. Success comes only to the extent that these business relationships are established and, more important, maintained. As anywhere, without continual reinforcement, relationships in Latin America have a short shelf life.

## MAKING A GOOD FIRST IMPRESSION

Without an initial good impression, you may not have the opportunity to proceed with your business. Therefore, you should make every effort to have your behavior conform to what is perceived in Latin American culture to be the dignified, polite and correct way to behave. You have only one opportunity to do this, so do not mess up. An unimpressive first impression in the United States might sometimes be mitigated by the facile use of language, which is unavailable to you in a Spanish-speaking country.

Here we will discuss the various adjustments that you might make to your appearance, and the protocols necessary to conduct yourself to increase the chances of success in Latin America, which may be different in at least some respects to your accustomed way of doing things. As is truly written, "The devil is in the details." These are the details!

Social or class distinctions are an important part of the Latin American culture, and these distinctions are established by a number of criteria. Racial background, education, physical appearance, deportment and attire are all computed as part of the calculus that determines your acceptability as a business associate. You have no control over your racial background, height or skin tones, but deportment and dress are two factors that, with care, you can use to your best advantage.

The importance of first impressions is even more significant in Latin America than it is in the States. An easygoing attitude, a winning smile and a great handshake will not carry you far in Latin America if you are not appropriately dressed. Latin Americans are all about formality in dress, manners and titles. The best impression is not based on your friendliness alone but rather is slowly developed through a trust relationship. Our stateside laid-back approach will be interpreted as frivolous and inappropriate in Latin America. Remember, this society is all about social distinctions.

## USE OF TITLES

Titles are extremely important in the Latin American culture and should be utilized at all times in both written and verbal communication. *No exceptions.* Not using them can mark you as culturally insensitive—in other words, an outsider.

First names are not utilized in Latin America as they are in the United States. This is a formal society. If you are invited to use a first name, wait until you receive the second invitation before doing so, and be sure to preface the first name with the appropriate professional title. Always err on the side of formality. If Licenciado Pedro Gómez insists that you call him Pedro, then call him Licenciado Pedro instead of Licenciado Gómez. Since a person might have a number of different appropriate titles, give preference to the professional title. The most common titles include:

**Professional Titles (Male and Female)**

- *Doctor (Dr.)* or *Doctora (Dra.)*: PhD or medical degree
- *Licenciado (Lic.)* or *Licenciada (Lic.)*: Bachelor of arts degree
- *Profesor*—Teacher at all levels. It is used for high school teachers and sometimes even elementary school faculty.
- *Contador Público (C.P.)*: Accounting degree
- *Ingeniero (Ing.)*: Bachelor of science or an engineering degree
- *Arquitecto*: Architect
- *Abogado*: Lawyer
- *Diputado (Dip.)* or *Diputada (Dip.)*: Elected public official

It is highly probably that most of the businesspeople you encounter will have a professional title, which you should use on every occasion, even if it feels clumsy or unnatural. During a meeting, if you have a college degree, you may be referred to simply as *Licenciado*, rather than using your given name. Don't look around surprised—they are talking to you. I have seen situations where a North American thought *Licenciado* was a Spanish first name. The use of a title alone is a normal way of addressing someone even among long-term friends.

Higher education is not common among the populace but is growing. The common use of academic titles such as *Licenciado* in one of the more unusual things noticed by North Americans. The chart below indicates that 23 percent of Latin Americans age eighteen to twenty-four were enrolled in some form of postsecondary education.

## Gross Higher Education Enrollment in Latin America and the OECD, 1965–2000

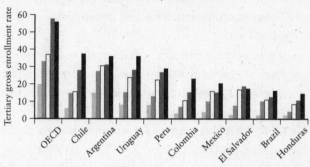

■ 1965 ■ 1975 ▢ 1985 ■ 1995 ■ 2000

Source: Task Force on Higher Education and Society (2000); World Bank (2002d).

Higher education still carries a lot of social status in Latin America, and its presence cannot be assumed, as we seem to do in the United States.

This chart shows the substantial growth in Latin American higher education enrollment with currently about 25 percent of Latin Americans enrolled in higher education. The Organisation for Economic Co-operation and Development (OECD) on the chart refers to an organization of thirty countries that enjoy high-income economies.

An individual who possesses a degree anticipates your acknowledgement of this high status.

### Personal Titles

In addition to professional titles in Latin America, we also utilize personal titles for those not qualified for a professional title. Rarely in social situations are personal titles utilized for those who have earned a professional degree. Personal titles include:

- *Señor (Sr.):* An adult male married or not
- *Señora (Sra.):* Any married or widowed woman. Sometimes older unmarried women are also addressed as *Señora*.
- *Señorita (Srta.):* Any unmarried female of any age
- *Don:* A term of real respect for an older man. You should use it only if he is introduced to you as *Don*. It supersedes all other titles.
- *Doña:* A term of respect for an older woman. Same practice as *Don*.
- *Maestro:* Used as a term of respect for competent people in their fields of endeavor. An excellent musician or a master carpenter might be addressed as *maestro*.

## Nicknames

Nicknames are common in Latin America and are freely utilized with good humor during ordinary conversation, with no offense given or taken. You will hear them affectionately used by associates in addressing one another, but as a visitor, you should avoid using them in a business setting. Just know that, no matter how racy nicknames may be, they are not intended as personal slurs among Latin Americans, as they tend to be in the United States.

In Latin America, the body is often perceived to be something very public and not private, as it is in the United States. Descriptive terms can and do come into play. Someone overweight might be called *gordo*, or fat, while someone underweight might be called *flaco*, or skinny, during business or social occasions. These terms are used with the utmost affection.

*Joven* has two distinct meanings. In a literal sense, it's any male adolescent, but it can also be used as a term of endearment for an elderly person with whom you are a very close friend. *Chico* or *chica* is an informal name for a young person, but it is also used as an endearment for the not so young. Some friend might address you with *"¿Qué pasa, chico?"* Which is loosely translated as "What's happening, buddy?" expressed in a very familiar sense. To which you would reply, *"Nada,"* which means "Nothing." This is an opening conversational gambit between people who know each other very well.

Diminutives are unique in Latin American cultural parlance and should be understood, although perhaps not used, by a visitor. They are another form of nickname, involving the practice of adding an *-ita* or *-ito* to names and virtually any other noun. *Carlos* is said to be *Carlitos* and *Margaret* is *Margarita*. Diminutives are used as a sign of familiarity and friendship. If you are addressed in this way, you'll know that you are considered one of the group.

A less commonly utilized opposite of this diminutive usage is the addition of *-sote* or *-sota*, which means "large." I am far from petite, and some of my friends, even in formal meetings, refer to me as *Doctor Kevinsote*. Not that there was a Kevinito with whom I might have been confused. However, notice that even in this case, the title is always used.

## SOCIAL GREETINGS

Latin Americans consistently utilize formal and stylized greeting formats. The Spanish equivalent of "hi" is not much used in the business or social vocabulary, even among friends. And there are some other distinct physical and linguistic customs by which you should abide.

**Handshake**

The Latin American rituals of meeting and departing require attention because they are unique to that culture. As a general practice, everyone shakes hands with everyone else at the beginning *and* the end of every formal or informal business or social encounter. This sometimes entails a lot of handshaking. It is easy to forget to do this, particularly upon departure from a group when the only contact you had with some people was the handshake upon arrival.

Even chance meetings in the street or in the hallway warrant a handshake. The physical touching is yet another way in which relationships are reinforced. Remember that the handshake is longer and firmer than customary in the United States. The stronger you are the more virile or macho you are taken to be, and the better suited for admission to an affinity circle. A gentler grip is considered effeminate and therefore less appealing in the macho Latin culture.

Women generally kiss each other on each cheek, although there are occasional handshakes at the beginning of a formal meeting. A woman encountering a man always shakes hands, unless she is more than a casual acquaintance. Under no circumstances should a man ever extend his hand to a woman, unless she puts her hand out first. If she leans forward to kiss his cheek, he should lean forward in a similar manner. If there is no initiation of physical contact by the woman—just say hello and smile.

**Besitos (Little Kisses)**

This is a form of embrace that women initiate in Latin America. It is somewhere between a handshake and an *abrazo* (see below) and is used between people of the opposite sex. Strangers rarely exchange *besitos*, although they can occur at the initial meeting between younger people. *Besitos* involve a light touching of the other person with your right hand, with your left hand by your side, and then a quick kiss past the right and left cheeks. You are essentially kissing air. This type of greeting is relatively uncommon during an initial business encounter, as it would be considered too forward on the part of the Latin American woman, but if you are well liked, it will be encountered in subsequent business meetings or on social occasions.

### *Abrazo* (Embrace)

The *abrazo* is the most unusual and occasionally awkward form of Latin American business and social contact. It involves two men of approximately the same social status embracing each other, with the right hand over the other man's shoulder, and pounding each other on the back. The number of hits is significant. Two gentle taps is reserved for someone you do not know well or like very much and is almost pro forma. Politicians from opposing parties who know but do not like each other do this. As your enthusiasm and friendship for the other person increases, the number and ferocity of the backslaps increases, to a maximum of four strong, mutual hits. The *abrazo* is reserved for the closest of friends and is always followed by a handshake.

The *abrazo* can be uncomfortable for many Americans since it isn't as commonly utilized in the United States as it is in Latin America. If your associate comes at you with arms open to perform an *abrazo*, reciprocate the embrace and give two gentle slaps on the back followed by a handshake. After a few experiences, it will become a natural and instinctive response for you. To ready yourself for the *abrazo*, keep your hands free at the end of any encounter. Do not pick up your briefcase until you have made your good-byes and are ready to walk out the door. Stay alert for what might be coming in the form of an embrace.

When first introduced to the president of the Mexican university where I served as dean, I quickly put out my hand for a strong handshake, but he was determined to share an *abrazo*, despite the fact that we didn't really know each other. He stepped enthusiastically into my outstretched hand, which caught him right below the belt buckle, knocking the wind out of him. Pick up your associate's clues and go with the flow. With a little experience, it will come naturally. If someone of higher social or economic importance offers you an *abrazo*, it is a sign of real friendship. Women don't use this form of greeting.

## THE LANGUAGE OF GREETINGS

Along with the handshake, a verbal greeting is normally anticipated in Latin America, even if you speak only minimal Spanish.

The morning greeting is *"Buenos días"* in Latin America, except in Brazil, where it is *"Olá."* These are used until exactly noon. Latin Americans are sensitive to these time constraints, and if you use the term after noon, someone will remind you of the correct time. Noon is always well heralded. Church bells ring and every radio station in Mexico plays the "Ave Maria" at the same time.

The afternoon greeting is *"Buenas tardes."* Note that this term is used until it is absolutely dark outside. In the summer, you may be wishing good afternoon at 7:30 p.m. if it is still light. This seems very strange to North Americans.

The nighttime greeting is *"Buenas noches,"* which is used until dawn.

After the greeting, you may hear *"¿Cómo está?"* or "How are you?" The proper response is *"Bien,"* or good, to which you might append *"¿Usted?"* meaning "You?" thereby asking your conversational partner how he is doing. He may then respond with *"Bien, bien, gracias a Dios,"* which means "Good, good, thanks to God." Then you had better move on to English before the situation gets out of hand and you become the recipient of an indecipherable torrent of Spanish, which you may or may not be able to survive.

## VERBAL COMMUNICATION TECHNIQUES

Conversation should focus on personal familiarity rather than business topics, which will eventually come into focus after relationships are firmly established. The topic of business is introduced by the client when he has reached his requisite comfort level. Usually this transition can take what is, for us, an inordinately long time, and it may not occur at all at the first meeting. Because business was not discussed, that does not mean the meeting was a waste of time—the contrary is quite often true. Smile and follow the lead of your potential client, who will certainly not sit there like a lump waiting for you to say something.

Latin Americans tend to be extroverted rather than reclusive. He might start out with inquiries about your travels and whether your wife accompanied you, which will lead into discussion of his family, whose pictures are likely to be on view in his office, so make sure that you pack some choice samples of your family in your wallet. Sports, the economy, the cost of things in the United States, and so on are favorite topics. Also, keep the following tips in mind:

- It is marginally better, in Latin American culture, to be married, because married people are perceived as being more stable and trustworthy and it gives you something important to share with your client, who almost certainly is married.
- Homophobia exists to a greater extent in Latin America than it does in the United States, so if you are homosexual, it might be in your business interest to keep this fact private.
- If you are divorced, there is no need to mention this, as divorce is frowned upon and seen as a personality defect. You can still discuss your children without mentioning your former partner.
- If you are single or without children to discuss, and an inquiry is made, just shrug, smile and say, "Hopefully someday!"
- It is to your advantage to appear as mature as you can. Younger people in Latin America are considered inexperienced and unreliable. For at least some of us, this maturity should not present a challenge. If you are lucky enough to appear youthful, you

might want to bring along someone older. Some young executives have an elderly coworker accompany them as the nominal head of the party.

Your demeanor should always be tranquil, smiling, never in a hurry, and you should never utter anything like "Let us get down to business." Contrary to conventional wisdom, you should never ask for a sale, even if it is the third visit. Your client is not stupid and knows why you are sitting there. Once you have established trust, he will ask you to do business with him.

## Topics to Avoid

**Politics.** Latin Americans generally like North Americans both personally and as a nation, but this affection does not necessarily extend to our politics. Traditionally they have little respect for any politician of whatever stripe, given their collective history. If you are pressed on a political issue, just shrug and say, "I didn't vote for him" and then attempt disengagement.

Avoid any discussion of Latin American politics and be wary of discussions of U.S. politics. The importance of this cannot be overemphasized, as engaging in this type of conversation is a common error. You will never know the real orientation of your prospective client, and you really cannot take a position on his concerns, because you have not walked in his shoes. You're likely to make judgments on some level without really knowing the facts.

**Smoking.** Smoking is prevalent in Latin America. Don't comment or demonstrate any distaste you might have.

Cancer statistics and other information concerning this practice are not topics for conversation. You are there to do business and not to improve Latin American health. Also, gasping for air, as a sign of your disapproval, is not a good idea, so suck it in or blow it out as the case may be. This can become awkward when you are averse to smoking but are honored with a present of a fine and expensive Cuban cigar after dinner. A possible response would be explaining that your doctor has forbidden your smoking.

# BODY LANGUAGE AND GESTURES

If you are not fluent in Spanish, then your communications must rely heavily on body language rather than on strictly verbal communication, which will be ineffective. We all know that gestures, facial expressions and posture all send messages. Without speaking Spanish, these actions may be the only way you can effectively communicate in circumstances when your prospective client does not speak any English. Everything that you communicate rests on the appropriateness of your nonverbal communication. Further complicating the matter, there are various physical gestures and attitudes that have a different significance in Latin America than they do in the United States, which visitors should be aware of.

### Physical Proximity

The major difference in body language universal throughout Latin America is in the domain of personal physical proximity. Close physical proximity is a general characteristic of the Latin American culture, as it is of most other cultures outside of the United States. North Americans tend to maintain a greater distance from one another than people in any other country in the world. You will soon notice how close Latin Americans stand together in line and how they walk close to one another, touching frequently.

If you are standing while talking with a client, try to keep yourself from unconsciously stepping back if he is too close for comfort. To do so would be considered rude. The client may unconsciously step up to you again. You will then be in the unenviable position of being slowly pursued around the room by your client. If he places his hand on your shoulder while speaking or even locks his arm through yours while walking, it is quite normal behavior.

We are accustomed to about fourteen inches of separation between people standing and facing each other. Latin Americans are accustomed to eight or nine inches. This makes a big difference in real-life situations. Practice this at home to get the feel of it. Latin Americans are very conscious of bodily and dental hygiene, and you should be too, which is not always easy in a hot and humid environment. Changing outfits at midday is not unheard of.

Try to seat yourself closer to your Latin American client than you would in the United States. If your chair is in front of his desk, pull it up until you almost touch the desk with your knees. Even advancing a few inches is symbolic and will be noticed by all present. Close physical proximity equals friendship in Latin America. The same is true around a coffee or conference table. In such circumstances, the most you can do is sit as close to your client as possible and then lean forward. Sitting back is considered to be standoffish.

## Facial Expressions

Avoid prolonged eye contact, which in most instances is considered aggressive. Intermittent and natural eye contact is good. It is appropriate to look at your client when it feels natural but avoid "the stare."

If you are the type of person with an unexpressive face or a naturally flat affect, you must attempt to combat this by trying to smile and nod as much as you can without appearing contrived. Your objective is to appear as interested as possible in your client's conversation, however unintelligible it might be to you, through the use of your facial expressions.

## Hand Gestures

In addition to the obviously vulgar hand signals common in the States, there are a number of other hand gestures, words and actions that are unacceptable in Latin America. The gestures listed below are widely utilized in Latin America, but are offensive in any business or professional setting. Keep this list in mind so you can avoid making any unintentionally rude gestures to your clients. The first two actions are the only ones you are likely to inadvertently perform as a normal part of your communication.

- Making the OK sign with your thumb to your index finger is vulgar. Placing the OK sign over your nose is a crude reference to homosexuality.

- Pointing your finger at someone or something is considered rude. To point out something, you purse your lips as if kissing and point your head in the direction you wish to indicate.
- Slapping your right fist into your open palm indicates aggression.
- Holding up your hand and wiggling your fingers at someone is obscene.
- Sticking your thumb between your middle and index finger with a closed fist is the equivalent of "giving someone the finger."
- Putting your hands in your pockets or on your hips is considered bad manners in Latin America.

### Mirroring

Reflecting your subject's posture, if skillfully done, is an excellent technique to increase his comfort level with you. This communication technique is the best practice in almost every situation, no matter where you might happen to be in our shrinking world. If your client begins to lean forward, you lean forward. If he gestures with his hands, you do the same. If he is sitting up straight, do not slouch.

## CHALLENGES FOR WOMEN IN BUSINESS

The position of women in the Latin American business culture is improving but still has a long way to go. For example, 52 percent of the college students in Mexico are women, and education, which is highly respected in the culture, is opening more and more doors for women. With increased higher education for women, their presence in Latin American business is only going to expand over time. There is evidence of real progress. For example, in South America there are two democratically elected women presidents—Michelle Bachelet in Chile and Cristina Fernández in Argentina—who happen to manage two of the most successful countries on the continent.

Gender discrimination is generally illegal in Latin America, but this is not to say that discrimination does not exist in the form of the infamous glass ceiling. Without strong family connections at the top of a particular corporate pyramid, it is very difficult for a woman to move to the higher echelons of business, and affirmative action is still an alien concept. When women are seen in the higher ranks in business, they are generally members of the family owning the business or related to some high-ranking political figure. A woman coming up through the ranks is highly unusual.

Problems that women must face go beyond breaking the glass ceiling. There are some commonplace activities that women might engage in in the United States that would not be a good idea in Latin America. Here are some commonsense suggestions for women traveling on business in Latin America:

- Among colleagues, never wear shorts, which are reserved for the beach. This is particularly true the farther south into Latin America you go or the farther out into rural areas you venture. If you are not on the job, wearing jeans is fine; otherwise avoid them.

- Streets are very rough, with many cracks and deep potholes. It is highly recommended, for your own safety, that you do not wear high heels.
- Avoid flashy jewelry.
- Do not drink alcohol, beyond a glass of wine, even if you are absolutely secure in your surroundings. This is both a safety and an etiquette issue. Polite women in Latin America do not drink more than a glass of wine (never beer), because women who drink are stereotyped as "party girls." Drinking with a male companion will almost certainly send a message, which you might not wish to send.
- Do not go out alone, especially at night.
- Feminism has yet to take hold in Latin America. Your persona should be firm, polite, reserved and unthreatening. Macho men can easily be threatened by a very bright, articulate woman. You may have a Harvard MBA and your client may not have graduated from high school, but it is not in your interest to make this evident.
- Do not go out to dinner with a Latin American male without a duenna or other companion. Try to invite his wife along, as she will be a perfect companion for you. Go alone and this will be misinterpreted, because if there is no escort, you are then a "couple" and you go out at your own peril.
- The same is true for riding in the front seat of a car. If you are traveling in your client's car, immediately head for the backseat, even if it's just the two of you. This is not an insult to him and is polite customary practice. If you sit in the front seat, it indicates that you are a couple.

- Stay calm and always be in command of your situation. Do not show emotions or fear.

## CLASS DISTINCTIONS

It's important to be aware that Latin America is a highly stratified culture. Socialization between the classes is very limited due to racial and economic factors. Some business travelers find this reality disquieting. Differences in the class structure are easily observed. At a high-end restaurant, the maître d' is tall and light-skinned, with a long nose and an elongated face. The kitchen helper is short and dark with a round face and a squat nose. You are unlikely to have any business relationships with individuals who have a high percentage of indigenous heritage.

## The Indigenous Population

Our cultural take on the North American indigenous population is quite different from Latin Americans' view of their indigenous populations. In our culture, the original Protestant settlers arrived from Europe with the general purpose of finding a place to live, making a good life and expanding their commercial interests. Intermarriage with the locals was almost unheard of. Native Americans were perceived as an impediment to this expansion process and were effectively marginalized if not actually exterminated.

The original Catholic invaders in Latin America came to find gold, which was a short-term and largely unsuccessful endeavor, and to convert the indigenous population to Catholicism. If you exterminated a population, you could not

convert them and save their souls. Intermarriage was common. It is highly probable that your potential client will be
at least partly descended from the original population. Para-
doxically, this aspect of the culture is virtually ignored or minimized in Latin America because the indigenous population
is considered to be backward if not unintelligent. Being of
partial indigenous heritage is something to be hidden rather
than celebrated as such heritage has, generally speaking,
come to be feted in the United States.

---

It is probable that you will encounter these class distinctions in one form or another during your visit, and you
should not react. It might take the form of blatant disre-
spect shown by your client toward an indigenous worker.
It is best to say nothing and keep a flat affect when faced
with such situations. Do not smile or nod, and don't agree.
In general, the managerial or middle classes, who have
a high percentage of European heritage, consider those
with a relatively high percentage of indigenous heritage
to be a rather ignorant, shiftless subclass. Remember, you
are there to further your commercial interests and not to
reform Latin American society. Stay focused!

When a problem arises, you might find your client
vehemently condemning his compatriots for their many
supposed inadequacies. Generally speaking, he is refer-
ring to the portion of the working class with a higher
percentage of indigenous heritage than his own and that
has aroused his ire. It is a big mistake, which I made on
one occasion, to point out that he also shares some of
this heritage.

# 6
# Getting Down to Business

*Toto, I've a feeling we're not in Kansas anymore.*
—Dorothy

The distance to Latin America is greater in mind-set than it is in miles traveled. Conventional wisdom says that it is difficult to do business south of the border. This is true, but only in the sense that you cannot conduct your business in Latin America as you would in the United States. We have covered this in detail in the preceding chapter. In Latin America you will experience a paradigm shift wherein business relationships are rooted in friendship and, most important of all, in personal trust. It requires an unequivocal commitment on your part to behave in whatever way is necessary to succeed in this environment. Now we will get down to the cultural minutiae that will, taken together, send the message that you are a serious, respectful person who has come to do serious business.

## BUSINESS CARDS

Business cards, formally designed on good white stock with black ink, are the norm and carry more importance in Latin America than they do in the United States. They will be intensely scrutinized by your business associates. If you can, avoid a big corporate logo in Day-Glo colors and graphics. It can make the card look like a low-end advertisement that lacks gravitas. Do what is necessary to keep your cards pristine. Design the card as formally as those produced by a high-end law firm. Your intended communication is that you are a serious person.

A small investment with a big return is a Spanish-only or double-sided bilingual card. Print your professional title in front of your name, for example, Lic. John Smith or C.P. Mary Jones. Abbreviations are fine. Your correct professional title is very significant because your title helps establishes who you are in the social pecking order. Put your corporate position in Spanish on the card. Be certain of the correct spelling and format. Utilize a printer who is aware of the nuances of a Latin American business card. A correct card communicates that you are a respectful and careful person.

When receiving a business card, don't immediately stick it in your pocket. Read it, as the prospective client will yours. It is helpful to repeat the name of the person giving it to you and, if appropriate, ask if you are pronouncing the name correctly. Make certain you leave your card along with a big smile with the secretary, whose name you should write down in your notebook. Expect to present her with a small gift on your next visit (see page 123 for more on gifts).

The presentation of your card is an opportunity to demonstrate yet another indication of respect for your client. After shaking hands, hold the card out with both hands, with the Spanish side facing the client. Have it ready to go and be cool about it. You should be standing, and a slight nod of the head when presenting the card is appropriate. Start with the most senior person present and go down the line. If you don't know who is senior, start with the person you think is oldest. *Never, ever drop the card on the table* in front of someone or deal the cards like a poker hand. This is considered very rude and disrespectful.

## BUSINESS ATTIRE

The way you look sends a loud and clear message in Latin American business circles. If you do not look the part, you cannot play the part. You are as you appear to be. Your clients will dress in the most stylish business fashion available to them at their income and professional level, and so should you.

Besides a few exceptions noted in Part Two, hot or cold, late in the evening or early in the morning, the only acceptable form of business attire for a manager is a dark suit, white shirt, and conservative tie. Working managers wear a two-piece suit, while the upper echelons wear a three-piece suit, rather than jeans and a polo shirt, which adorn some of our highest corporate managers. Slacks or sports jackets are not worn by upper management. Office workers typically display a white shirt and tie. If they have a sports jacket, it is customarily left over the back of their office chair. If you arrive looking like the office messenger, you will be accorded that status.

Unlike in the United States, where informality seems to be a growing trend, a Latin American office worker's appearance can give you a valuable clue to his position in the corporate hierarchy. Rank requires a certain dress code. For example, at Latin American universities, deans customarily wear a suit, while the faculty make due with a jacket and tie. This same business dress code is used in much of the world, particularly in Asia. Casual Friday simply does not exist in the traditional Latin American culture.

Your shoes should have a high polish. Streets are dusty, but there are individuals, many of them quite young, on street corners to polish shoes. It is one of the professions that enable the very poor, who are in the vast majority in Latin America, to put bread on the table, as there is no version of our social security or aid to children in any Latin American country except Uruguay. Have your shoes shined each day. Do not buy a new pair before you begin your travels, as you will be on your feet much of the time and you need to be comfortable. If you are at a high altitude, there will also be a tendency for your feet to swell a bit, which will make even your day-to-day shoes seem tighter. Altitude is an important consideration for women, who experience more difficulties with stylish shoes than men do.

Neat beards are OK, but the unshaved look will immediately destroy your credibility. Ponytails are reserved for artistic types. Latin American males are also fastidious about their fingernails, and many managers wear clear nail polish. Blend in as best you can.

The rules for women's business attire are basically the same as in the States. One caution, however: the streets you walk on may be slate, cobblestone, raised pavement or worse, so make sure you pack a pair of shoes with low heels. Also keep your good jewelry at home.

## SCHEDULING AN APPOINTMENT

Be aware when you establish your schedule that your meetings probably won't start punctually and there is usually no scheduled time for conclusion. It's over when it is over. There may be no explanation given or even an apology for a late start. This is normal because no one, except the occasional clueless North American, anticipates that meetings will actually start on time. A twenty-minute delay is normal, and up to an hour's delay is not uncommon but *you must never be late*. Be prepared for these scheduling practices and don't schedule your meetings tightly. Smile, hang in there and enjoy your coffee. Stay focused!

Upon your arrival, the meeting may be canceled, and you must provide for such an eventuality in your scheduling. This is not an uncommon occurrence, so don't take it as a personal affront or show any disappointment. Someone's child may be sick or another family situation may have arisen. Family always comes first in Latin America. Simply reschedule and stay cool. This is the reason you have provided for the unscheduled day left at the end of your trip, to cover such contingencies.

Latin Americans, with few exceptions, treat appointments as tentative until you are actually in town, because of the long lead time between setting the appointment and the meeting itself. Historically, there have been a lot of no-shows by North American business visitors. In addition to confirming your appointment a week before your departure, you should telephone your client and announce your arrival as soon as you get to your hotel. Make sure that both he and his secretary know where you are staying, in case of changes in schedule.

## Ideal Appointment Times

Optimally, try to schedule your appointments on Tuesday through Friday from 10 a.m. to 12:30 p.m. Before 10 a.m., your client is unlikely to be present; he'll be either otherwise engaged in a business breakfast or catching up with his own business. At 2 p.m., everyone goes out for a long *comida*. Returning at 4 p.m.—and we are assuming just a two-hour *comida*, even though they sometimes run much longer—people tend to move and think in slow motion for the remainder of the day, although they do work late into the evening. These are not good hours for meetings. In reality, you can conclude that you will probably hold only one business meeting per day, unless you can snag a breakfast meeting. Meetings generally start late and run long. Count on it. If your client sends you out the door quickly, this is usually a sign that he has just granted you a courtesy visit out of respect for his friend who recommended you. There is no business there for you, so move on.

Meetings are also open-ended, because it would be impolite for your Latin American host to schedule a time to stop talking with his North American friend. You must never appear rushed or harried, because you have all the time in the world for your new acquaintances. When scheduling, you cannot reliably count on travel time from one location to the other due to traffic and the other realities of Latin American life, which include, among other things, strikes, demonstrations, auto accidents and religious processions ad nauseam. It will inevitably take longer than you anticipated, and you must be able to accept the offer of *comida* with your business associates if it is made, or be able to invite them to *comida*. Their acceptance is a portent of good things to come.

Due to environmental considerations, your energy level will not be what it is in the United States, and you will need to schedule an occasional break. Altitude, jet lag, different food and water and interrupted sleep cycles are common factors that result in your functioning at less than 100 percent. Don't push yourself. Even for experienced travelers in this environment, exhaustion appears to be the rule rather than the exception. Business travel is neither glamorous nor restful.

## Latin American Work Schedules

Latin American work schedules must also be considered when scheduling your appointments. Work in the traditional mode usually begins at 8 a.m. and lasts until 2 p.m. Then there is *comida*. Work resumes at 4 p.m. and ends at 8 p.m. On Saturday, Latin Americans work from 9 a.m. until 1 p.m. Banks are open only in the mornings, from Monday to Friday. The banking system is slowly evolving in the large cities with longer bank hours and evidence of a less personal style under pressure from increasing commercial traffic and the gradual introduction of North American business practices. Restaurants and retail shops remain open but other businesses close for *comida*.

There are also many holidays, both official and unofficial, to take into consideration when planning appointments. Most people take off Holy Week and the time between Christmas and New Year's, along with the Three Kings and numerous other national and religious holidays, in addition to personal birthdays and vacation time. Sometimes when one of these many holidays falls on Tuesday or Thursday, it is an excuse for a four-day weekend, similar to our Friday after Thanksgiving. There is also summer vacation. In South America (e.g., Brazil, Argentina, and Chile), the seasons are reversed and summer vacation is taken in January or February. Carefully check the local calendars, which can be found on the official webpage for each country, and avoid meetings not only on the holidays but also on the days immediately preceding and following. See Appendix B for a full list of national and religious holidays that are typically observed in Latin America.

## The Term "Gringo"

The legends concerning the word "gringo" require a bit of explanation. As told to me by a Mexican business associate, this appellation originated during one of our periodic invasions of Mexico. The U.S. troops supposedly wore green uniforms, and the locals stood by the roadside and shouted, "Green, go home." This fable is certainly just that, and Wikipedia provides a great article on the topic, with no real conclusion as to the origin of the term.

Historically the term "gringo," whatever its origin, has been considered a very negative term. What is true is that after World War II, North Americans living in Mexico began to use the term to describe themselves, so the word lost its sting. However, on occasion, when a Latin American utters the word with a snarl, it reverts to being a negative term. It still can mean an unwelcome North American, and this is something you want to mitigate at every available opportunity.

## TALKING BUSINESS

We talked a bit in the previous chapter about the essential step of communicating with your client before any business is ever discussed. There will come a time, however, when your client is ready to start talking shop. Wait for your client to decide when the conversation should shift over to business. When it does, there are some key issues that you will be faced with and need to be aware of.

If your client speaks limited English or you are using a translator, follow some commonsense rules when communicating. First, be aware of your volume. We all have a tendency to shout when we think someone does not understand us. Face your client directly, speaking just slightly louder than a conversational tone. Speak slowly, but not too slowly, which can sound patronizing. Speaking too loudly has the same effect. Speak too quickly, and even if your client has some English skills, you will lose his comprehension and perhaps even that of your translator. This is a particular problem for New Yorkers, whose rate of speech tends to be faster than the norm. Keep your head up and do not mumble down into your notes.

Use short, simple sentences with *no idioms*, and pause for a few seconds every minute or two to give your client time to digest your meaning and to respond. If there are no responses, you will need to try another tactic. Use a white board to illustrate your point if there is one in the office, as this may help, especially with numbers.

At the conclusion of the meeting do the following:

- Have a short document ready with your main talking points simply stated, for presentation after the meeting. Prepare this ahead of time, and if you have the time, it is an excellent idea to have the translator make a Spanish-language copy of this document.
- Thank your client profusely and sincerely for his time and courtesy. Give a simple smile and say, *"Te agradezco el tiempo que me dedicaste"* or *"Muchas gracias por tu tiempo"* or *"Te doy gracias por dedicarme tu tiempo."* Using the informal *tu* and *te* rather than the formal *usted* for the word "you" signals that you, at least, think that you and the client are friends.

## YOUR SALES CYCLE

The sales process is exasperatingly slow in Latin America, and many people give up their venture there believing that they will never make progress. This is one of the major impediments to doing business in Latin America. If you cannot accept these prolonged time frames, then consider saving your time and money and don't go. It may take several meetings before you make any appreciable progress. The phrase used to describe this environment is *nada es fácil*, "nothing is easy," and a Latin American business venture is not for the insecure or faint of heart. There are few fast closes. This is a long-term relationship-building project.

You must adapt to this extended cycle because the potential benefits of doing business in Latin America are substantial, and you do not have any choice if you want to enter this market. This is a thriving youthful environment for you to explore, with tremendous prospects for explosive growth in the future.

The land is rich and the seas productive. The working-class poor remain repressed, but the society itself is wealthy. There are more billionaires per hundred thousand people in Mexico than in any other country in the world. Carlos Sims, arguably one of the richest men in the world, is Mexican. By comparison, Warren Buffett and Bill Gates are relatively impoverished, perhaps due to their philanthropy. Substantial charitable donations by the superwealthy are less common in Latin America than in the United States. Foundations, or *patronados*, are not a highly significant element in the culture.

The North American economy and living standards are envied. The *otro lado*, or the other side of the river, is the land of opportunity and an object of admiration. American products have the reputation of being of high quality and "in." In this, and most other respects, seeking business for American products is a downhill battle for you.

## YOUR COMPETITION

You have a significant advantage over your competitors from other countries if your merchandise is made in the USA. This is considered an indication of quality. Competing with other U.S. companies comes down to relationships, all other factors, such as price, being essentially equal. If they know you and trust you, the business is yours!

In most Latin American countries, U.S. goods enter duty-free, while there are substantial customs duties on many goods from Europe and Asia. The absence of duty more or less compensates the buyer for the lower prices usually charged by your competitors.

The Chinese are reputed to dump even lower-quality merchandise in Latin America than they do in the United States. These extremely cheap imports destroy the nascent local industries. It is also true that China is not being receptive to Latin American exports. Cecilio Garza-Limón, in his article in the April 30, 2007, issue of the *Latin Business Chronicle*, states that the ratio of imports from China to exports to that country has reached 31 to 1. In response, Mexico has become protectionist and at least to some extent punitive with Chinese goods. According to Sr. Garza, "The Ministry of Commerce imposed compensatory fees on more than 6,000 dutiable Chinese items, many of them not even produced in Mexico and therefore not threats. Other Chinese imports had surcharges of up to 1,000 percent." However, according to the article, Chinese goods are still marketed in Mexico to a considerable extent as contraband permitted entry by corrupt customs officers. This situation with cheap Chinese goods is not unique to Mexico and is mirrored in other Latin American countries.

The absence of duty under NAFTA gives U.S. goods a competitive advantage in Mexico, and other free trade agreements offer similar, if less all-encompassing, benefits. The same is true for the other side of the transactions. The absence of duty on Latin American goods entering the United States keeps the prices of such merchandise lower than goods imported from countries not enjoying duty-free status. Therefore goods purchased in Mexico and sold in the United States also have a competitive advantage. Latin America provides all of us with a win-win situation.

## COMMON BUSINESS ROADBLOCKS

The North American businessperson will face a number of unexpected challenges during any typical Latin American business transaction. All constitute impediments in the commercial process. The issues center around both communication styles and the cultural assumptions Latin Americans make in their business relationships, which are in many respects different from your normal ways of thinking about and doing things. No matter how you're used to doing business at home, keep the following possible mistakes involving cultural nuances in mind and adapt to your host country's business style.

### Not Working on the Right Scale

We tend to talk "big" because our culture has conditioned us to think that big is better. The Latin American businessperson is thinking "small" is safer. All Latin American countries are smaller and much poorer than the United States. In recent memory, most of them have gone through horrific economic upheavals and devaluations of currency, which effectively destroy the savings and capital of individuals and companies. This is exacerbated in the current market by the utter dependence of Latin American countries on the U.S. economy, where this sort of economic upheaval is now happening to a lesser extent as well. It has been said that when the United States sneezes, Latin America catches pneumonia. Just a few examples:

- The 1994 economic crisis in Mexico, also referred to as the Mexican peso crisis, was triggered by the sudden devaluation of the Mexican peso. In effect, overnight the pesos held by Mexicans became essentially worthless. This was related to an economic downturn in the United States.
- Venezuela's inflation rate reached an annual 30.9 percent in 2008, which was an eleven-year high, making imports out of the reach of most Venezuelans. Most manufactured goods were imported, and so they have become exceptionally expensive. The turmoil is blamed by the Venezuelans on U.S. imperialism and repression.
- The Argentine economic crisis affected Argentina's economy during the last decade with hyperinflation and a general decrease in economic activity resulting from trade imbalances with the United States.
- Brazil is the eighth-largest economy in the world and is heavily dependent on purchases by the United States. As the U.S. economy falters, Brazilian exports are affected and the economy becomes stagnant.

Because of historic economic and political uncertainty, businesspeople in Latin America are much less willing to take a risk, and big plans involve big risks. Experience has taught Latin Americans to believe that the economic past repeats itself and that there is no great hope in the future. Their attitude is "Let us see what we can do with the here and now." This attitude is reinforced by the fact that many midsize businesses are family owned and operated and are therefore focused on immediate results rather than decades-long development projects. Corporations tend to have distant horizons and are more willing to take a long-range risk than a family operation.

So think small and scale down your volume and, more important, your rhetoric. If business works out and you have earned a new client, bigger things will come along for you. Skip the grandiose blather about covering all of Latin America with your product and thereby making your Latin American partner incredibly rich. Latin Americans greet such claims with justifiable derision.

For example, if you are selling a manufacturing system, emphasize that the client can choose to purchase only one machine in the process, which will increase productivity. This means that you will return with a contract, albeit a diminutive one. For this, your peers may consider the trip a failure, but based on the knowledge you have acquired from this book, you know it has been an outstanding success. Trust has been established and doors are opening.

If you are selling seeds, suggest only a minor quantity for testing purposes. No matter how persuasive you are or how elaborate your presentation, the conservative family farmer, no matter how vast his holdings, is unlikely to take even a minor risk.

## Going Too Fast

Patience is an essential virtue in Latin America. Nothing is accomplished quickly. If it is perceived that you are rushing the business, you will be reinforcing the negative North American stereotype. Nobody likes pressure, particularly when it originates from a foreigner. You might be anxious to do business quickly and return home, but your client is not, and he will sense that you are patronizing him if you're obviously impatient with his reluctance to move forward. Slow down and eventually you will do more business.

## Not Following Up

The follow-up is as significant as the initial meeting, if not more so. Failure to follow up expeditiously means that the initial meeting was a waste of your time and money. Inadequate attention to this segment of the sales cycle is the major reason for failure and the major reason that Latin America is considered a difficult market in which to do business. Not only will you be required to follow up, but you will need to do multiple meetings in relatively short order.

Face-to-face is the only way to do an effective follow-up. The time between meetings optimally should be about two weeks; certainly no more than a month should elapse between contacts. If you are unable to follow up in person, weekly calls to elevate the client's level of awareness are necessary. The phone also helps to remind your client that you are on your way down for the next personal visit. Chat for a while and ask about family. Unless you are faxing information that your client needs in order to move forward with the project, this type of communication is unlikely to have much of an effect for following up, but this unacceptable alternative may be the only option available to you.

**Taking Promises Literally**

Don't become resentful of your client's lack of follow-up to promises made. This can result in your discouragement. Statements to the effect that "I will sign this and get it off to you next week" will be quickly made to you, and noncompliance doesn't necessarily mean the client doesn't want to do business. This is the Latin American culture. Everything moves slowly.

What should you do? Being aggressive and pushing the issue will not help your cause and in fact will hurt it because of the stereotype of the aggressive North American. Just waiting for something to happen will not help your cause, because you will simply fade into the woodwork. The only options for you are patience and persistence. You've recognized since its conception that this will be a long-haul project and so you have prepared yourself for what seem to you to be unconscionable delays. Your persistence will eventually be rewarded. Regular follow-up visits and at least weekly communication in the intervening periods will eventually result in success. It is a function of your intuition and good business sense.

If months go by and you cannot get an appointment after repeated attempts, then you might conclude that this client is not for you at this point in time and move on. You should, however, keep up the drip mail campaign and attempt to set an appointment with the client each time you are in the area.

**Procrastination**

This is one of the great cultural characteristics of Latin America. When asked what this means to her, Luz Amelia McClellan of ServiTrans in Mexico City responded,

"Having to repeat one's self, having to reconfirm several times, having to explain what my definition of professional means, which includes a huge attention to details." Perhaps this habit originates in the relaxed cultures of southern Europe, which then migrated to Latin America. This cultural quirk is the reason you confirm and reconfirm appointments.

This may not seem like a very efficient way to do business, and it is not. Chaos is part of the culture. Lack of long-term or even short-term planning is quite common, and everything is done at the last possible minute, or *a última hora*.

In response to a missed commitment on your client's part, you may be met with the response of "Mañana." This can mean many things, among them literally "Tomorrow" or "Later" or "I don't know," or perhaps even "Never." Your client may be too polite to tell you that he doesn't want to do business and so "Mañana" becomes his catchall response of convenience. Which meaning is intended by your host? There is no way for you to really know, except to wait. After a series of such "Mañana" responses, you will get the message that you are on indefinite hold. Move on.

## Not Understanding Financial Practices

Be very careful when accepting a check from anyone in Latin America. In these countries, proffering a check with insufficient funds is a serious criminal offense equal to robbery of the amount involved and is seldom attempted, because of the draconian laws. What is done is "accidentally" presenting you with a defective check, which is "broken" in the sense that it will not be honored by the bank. The person who gives you the check knows that, but you do not! A very tiny piece of paper torn off the corner of a check will invalidate the document. The same is true for erasures or changes of any kind, no matter how insignificant. There are also complex rules on how the amount must be indicated in Spanish on the check, which change from country to country and even bank to bank. For example, should the centavos, each of which is a hundredth part of a peso, be written out, or indicated with numerals on a check? A mistake such as this makes the check valueless. With an invalid check, you are then put in the position of exchanging something of value for a worthless piece of paper, without any possible recourse to the legal system, since you were naive enough to accept invalid paper. The person who gave you the check will by then have become unavailable for a replacement.

It is not easy to protect yourself in this matter, and experience is a very expensive teacher. Your greatest risk comes from a check received from an individual or small businessperson, as major corporations do not usually engage in fraud. Here are some options to protect yourself:

- Have the person proffering the check meet you personally at *his* bank. Take the check and deposit it immediately, to make sure it clears, and then either take the proceeds in cash or have that bank transfer the funds to your bank.
- Accept payment with a cashier's check.
- Accept cash on the spot only at *your* bank. Have your banker authenticate the local currency and deposit it directly into your account.

Be very careful.

The same is true of local currency. If there is a tiny tear or a bit missing from a corner of the bill, most vendors won't accept the currency. Replacement involves a trip to the bank and a long line. You are likely to encounter this situation, since local vendors try to pass off these "broken bills" on unsuspecting visitors, thus saving themselves a trip to the bank. When enmeshed in this, I try to use a piece of clear tape to cover the defect and pass the money off at the first opportunity.

Be careful with the local money because many countries (Bolivia, Chile, Colombia, Uruguay, Mexico and Argentina) call their currency the peso. Each of these pesos has a different value against the dollar and is not interchangeable with any other. Sometimes the local banks will not exchange these foreign pesos for the local variety. Rapid inflation can occur, and governments can arbitrarily change the value of their country's peso against the dollar.

In transferring and exchanging money, always use your credit card wherever you can. For pocket cash, make sure your ATM pin number is only four characters, as many machines outside the United States do not accept a PIN longer than this. The exchange rate given by ATMs is the same as the bank rate used by the credit card companies and is a far better rate than anything you can get from the exchange houses. This will also ensure that you won't get local counterfeit bills. The worst place for foreign exchange is paying in U.S. dollars at hotels and restaurants.

All business transactions involving foreigners are conducted in dollars, as explained later in this section.

In street transactions, the vendors prefer dollars and will usually provide a discount to receive them, but they will offer the change from the transaction in local currency. Use this change before you leave or you will eventually accumulate five pounds of local currency, which will be brought home with you and become useless. Banks in the United States are reluctant to exchange foreign currency for dollars unless the amounts involved are substantial. They will not exchange coins.

In the local newspapers, you will see the prices of property for sale termed in dollars. This is illegal for the Latin American vendor, but it is common business practice. A contract written in dollars can be challenged in court on that basis, except in the few countries in which the dollar is legal currency. See your lawyer before signing anything.

If someone insists on doing business with you only in the local currency, you must insistently and persistently demur and require a dollar transaction, otherwise you could wind up with a substantial amount of local currency that, due to a devaluation, is worth far less that you believed it to be when you accepted it. This local currency scam in various guises is foisted upon the unwary. If you are offered cash in U.S. dollars, be careful of counterfeit.

This issue with local currency presents some serious difficulties with a sales contract. You may be thinking in dollars and your counterpart might be responding in terms of dollars, but when the contract is produced you will magically find it written in the local currency. It will be explained to you that under the law all contracts must be written in the local currency, which is true. If you sign this contract, it presents a risk for you, as the relationship between the local currency and the dollar may change before payment is made. Quick execution minimizes this risk, but that is not always possible. Your only recourse is to make certain that the exchange rate to be used for payment is specified in the contract. Look carefully for this clause and have your lawyer check it over.

In the first half of this chapter we have gone through the process of actually getting down to business, and in the second half we discussed some of the problems that might be encountered during the process. Being prepared is the necessary first step in success. Now that the meetings are covered, we'll move on to an equally—if not more—crucial part of your journey: dining and entertainment.

# 7
# Entertaining and Giving Gifts

*Americans who travel abroad for the first time are
shocked to discover that despite all the progress
that has been made in the last 30 years, many
foreign people still speak in foreign languages.*
—Dave Barry

Entertaining and shared meals with your clients are
vital to your success. If you have never shared at least
one *comida*, which is a vital element in business relationships with your client, you are highly unlikely to secure
business with him. In fact you should expect to share
*comida* after each of your subsequent visits, which you
should conveniently schedule for about 11 a.m. This is
where relationships are built. It really does not matter
who eventually picks up the check, and such matters are
discussed later in this chapter. After-hours socializing is
unusual in that Latin Americans work long hours and,
except for very special occasions, prefer to then be home
with their families.

The rules and traditions of Latin American entertaining and gift giving are significantly different in many
aspects from our North American customs. The meals
themselves are different, the etiquette is European and

the list of acceptable and unacceptable mealtime topics must be understood. The type and particularly the presentation of gifts take on special significance in your efforts to become a member in good standing of your affinity circle. As indicated earlier, the more of an effort you make to fit in, the more you will be accepted.

## BUSINESS DINING

### Table Manners

Table manners in Latin America are not only different from those in North America, they are *much more* important in that they are considered to be a visible representation of your culture and level of education. Latin Americans utilize European- rather than American-style table manners, whereas we follow the Continental style. The European style of eating is believed to be evidence of the cultural sophistication of the region—something you should aim to project. Below are some etiquette tips to keep in mind when dining with your colleagues:

- Hold your knife in your right hand and your fork in your left. They do not switch places as they do in the United States.
- Do not keep your hands concealed in your lap, but rather keep them visible, when dining. Have your wrists resting on the edge of the table and keep your elbows off the table.
- Take small bites and chew slowly. Chewing loudly, clanging silverware or scraping the plate is considered even more vulgar in Latin America than it is in the United States.

- After you have cut your food, position your knife so that the tip of the blade is resting on the plate and the handle is lying on the table.
- Cross your knife and fork on the plate when you are finished eating.
- Your client will normally sit at the head of the table. You will be seated to his immediate right. When you are the host, give the seat at the head of the table to your senior Latin American contact. *Seating is not random* and is sometimes indicated by place cards, but more likely you will be shown to your seat by a subordinate. Do not sit down until you are invited to sit.
- When your client proposes a toast to you, stand and always propose another toast in return, to which he might reciprocate ad nauseam. The normal toast is "*Salud.*" Be sure you drink after the toast is made and before you put your glass back down on the table. Not to do so is considered an insult because it indicates that you did not like the client's toast.

## Buen Provecho

This term means "good eating." As you enter a restaurant, it's customarily mumbled to every table you pass—whether or not you know the people—along with a slight nod and eye contact that is reciprocated. After the food has been placed on your table, it is also vocalized by the host to your table-mates and constitutes an informal signal to begin eating. This salutation effectively establishes a connection or relationship between everyone eating at the table and in the restaurant.

No longer are we strangers. This practice provides an excellent demonstration of your cultural sensitivity and marks you as an "insider." When leaving, it is *"Buen gusto."* Join in . . . it feels good.

---

## Types of Meals
The business meal is where relationships are built and your behavior evaluated. If you never go out for a meal with your client, there is probably no business for you with him.

- *Desayuno,* **or breakfast.** Breakfast starts about 8 a.m. and may last two hours. Business breakfasts are becoming more common with increasingly sophisticated businesspeople in largely urban areas. It is a quick, alcohol-free occasion with a more or less fixed ending time.
- *Comida,* **or lunch.** *Comida* is the most common form of business entertainment, although it in no way resembles our noon lunch experience. Usually *comida* starts about 2 or 3 p.m. and lasts two hours, but it can easily last much longer. Alcohol consumption at *comida* is normal.
- *Cena,* **or Dinner.** Dinner usually starts after 8 p.m. It is not a very common form of entertaining, except in Brazil. Latin Americans typically are family men who want to be home with their families. A dinner is more common if you have a spouse in tow and your host can bring his partner and make a night of it. Sometimes a show and dancing are added.

**What to Eat**

The food that you see will be divided into two categories. First will be the cuisine served at international hotels, and it is very much like what you are served at home. The local cuisine tends to be represented in these restaurants but will not be particularly appetizing for your guests, as it has been modified for international clientele.

The second category is the local cuisine, which varies from country to country and even within particular regions of each country. For example, just as you are not likely to find hush puppies served in Maine, you are not likely to find *mole* in abundance outside of Oaxaca, Mexico.

In general, the big difference between local Latin American restaurants and the hotel restaurants is that the food is spicier (or *picante*) at the local restaurants. The cuisine is based on the corn tortilla rather than on our wheat bread or potatoes. Dessert is not much appreciated but is served to foreigners and their guests. If a choice is available for a business meal, head for a restaurant serving local specialties, which demonstrates your acceptance of the culture. Ordering characteristic American hamburger fare is not good form.

When selecting wine at a meal, look to the locally produced vintages. In Mexico, Argentina and Chile they are quite good. Except for the Chileans, who are justifiably proud of their vintages, your clients might disparage their local wines, but they will be pleased if you prefer their local product. It is also a lot less expensive because the import duty on alcoholic beverages in Latin America is outrageous.

Accept what you are offered to eat even if you don't

like it or are not hungry. In any circumstance, don't refuse an offer of coffee, even if it looks and tastes like tar. It will be taken as an affront. There is a stereotype to be overcome of North Americans who stick up their noses at the local cuisine. The food will generally be good, if a little bit unusual, and perhaps more *picante* or hot than your customary diet. If you are in Oaxaca, Mexico, your hosts will be sure to put a plate of fried grasshoppers before you. It is a local specialty. Be a sport and eat a few, which sort of taste like salty peanuts. In Mesoamerica, you may be presented with *cuy*, which is roasted guinea pig—head, fur, feet and all.

You may be presented with other "off our menu" type dishes in other countries and cities. Just take a few mouthfuls and smile. You might discover that you actually like the stuff. The same is true for the worm at the bottom of a bottle of mescal. To be offered the worm is an honor, as it is believed to be an aphrodisiac, so slurp it down with a smile.

## Choosing a Restaurant

Generally speaking when someone invites you, he chooses the restaurant and pays the bill. When you are inviting, the best policy is to ask your clients to recommend a "good place" to eat, although they may insist on paying for the meal if they have recommended the restaurant. It is almost a universal instinct in Latin America to offer to provide food for guests at your own expense.

When circumstances demand it and you are selecting a place to eat, whether formal or informal, a good rule to follow when selecting a local restaurant, either for entertainment of guests or for personal consumption, is the "locals rule." If the place is frequented by many locals, the food probably merits joining the crowd. The opposite is even more suggestive. If an eating establishment is nearly deserted, pass it by regardless of the recommendation it has received or the number of stars awarded.

## Do You Drink the Water?

The water and coffee that you are offered during a meeting will be fine. Do not make a fuss, which is not very polite, or even an inquiry. The water is either straight out of a bottle or drawn from a purified filter. In a restaurant, you will normally be offered bottled water. If not, ask for it.

Those with delicate stomachs and/or anyone traveling outside the large urban areas should stick to bottled water, which is ubiquitous. You will find it in your hotel room and on the street corners. Avoid drinking tap water or using it to brush your teeth, because it can be bacteria-laden and will not taste pleasant due to the local purification processes. Inquire about the ice at restaurants, although even the most elaborate restaurants will sincerely assure you that their water for ice is purified at the local ice plant and comes bagged to the kitchen. Stay with containerized drinks such as beer and soda, drunk directly from the container, if the situation permits it, thus avoiding contamination on the glass. A stomach problem can destroy your trip.

Don't make a big fuss over the water. It is not a gracious thing to do and transforms you into a negative stereotype. If you have a concern, valid or not, be extremely circumspect about it. It is not that the water is necessarily bad. Local inhabitants drink the water and seem to do fine, and contrary to conventional folklore, they are subject to the same intestinal afflictions that we are, although they may have acquired some immunity to the local bacteria. In any case, it is prudent to pack a supply of stomach medicine for use in the event you are stricken.

## Restaurant Service

There is, among North Americans, a misconception about the speed of service in Latin American restaurants. First, realize that the food is cooked to order rather than taken from a hot table or microwave, so preparation takes a bit longer. Secondly, no one there is in a particular hurry.

The real delay is the length of time it takes to receive your check. No restaurant in Latin America will ever bring you a check until you specifically request it, unlike most restaurants in the United States, where the check will sometimes be placed on the table with your coffee before you have finished the meal. In our high-end restaurants, waiters often hover, check in hand, prompting you to ask for it, pay and leave.

Tipping is the same as in the United States, with 15 to 20 percent being the norm in the good restaurants. Even if service is awful, which is unlikely, leave 10 percent. Stiffing the waiter is unacceptable.

Latin Americans are very courteous people, and it would be considered rude on their part to prematurely present a check as if they wanted you to actually leave. You can sit in most restaurants until the end of days and no one will bring a check until it is requested. Meanwhile the clueless traveler is sitting there, unhappy with the delay, waiting for the check to be presented.

There are many terms for "the check" in Spanish, but a ploy that works anywhere in the world is to catch the attention of the waiter and make a little scribbling action against your left palm, or you might say, *"La cuenta, por favor,"* which means "Check, please."

**Paying the Bill**

If you are with a group, there is usually a wrestling match among the participants after the meal as to who pays the check. Sometimes it seems excessive by our standards and even a bit silly, but it is carried out with good humor. It's the way they play their game. Why make such a fuss? It is a macho thing to pay the bill, and in winning this small social battle, they have proved that they are more macho than you are. If you were the person invited, concede after a pro forma attempt at the check, and let the others wrestle over the bill. The waiter will always hand the bill to the local resident, which does not help your cause.

Who pays if you issue the invitation? Expect the same wrestling match and check grabbing *if* you let it get to that point. Slip the waiter your credit card before the meal. This is normal business practice and your card will be secure. When the waiter brings you the check, sign and then smile at everyone. In this way, you are both macho and *simpático*.

Remember, when paying for anything in a restaurant or store, do not place your credit card or cash on the table or counter, but rather place it in the hand of the person who is serving you, as this action establishes a connection between you. It is a small matter, but a significant signal that you have good manners and are culturally sensitive.

## HOME ENTERTAINMENT

The invitation to a Latin American home for dinner is not typical in this tight-knit family-oriented society. The exception being a *fiesta* (or party), which might run the gamut from a simple birthday party for one of the children to a wedding.

It could be a *quinceañera*, which occurs when a daughter reaches fifteen years of age. This is a big affair similar to our social coming-out parties, and it is staged on the scale of a wedding. If you are in the United States when you receive the invitation to any such affair, you must make every effort to go back for this party and bring your spouse if possible, as it is an honor to be invited. The celebration is very formal. If it's impossible for you to attend, profound apologies and a really nice gift are appropriate. Since you are dealing with a fifteen-year-old girl, some sort of name-brand fashionable item would be appropriate.

You are not expected to arrive on time for any social event except as noted below. For a party, being one hour late is normal, and for dinners, thirty minutes is OK. Arrive earlier and you might find the host still dressing. As during the day, the dress tends to be formal, with suit and tie being the norm for men, even if it is very hot. Remember to shake hands with everyone you encounter except the servants.

The only time this tardiness rule does not apply is the rare invitation that indicates the term *a punto* or "English time" after the time. This means that the host expects the event to start at the stated time.

Holidays are an excellent excuse for a celebration, as

are World Cup games. Should you ever be invited, *you must go*, because it means that you are among a circle of friends. Always bring a gift. Flowers, alcohol and candy are all acceptable.

---

**Bullfighting** is popular throughout most parts of Latin America, and you may be invited on a Sunday to accompany your client to a fight. This is a mark of real friendship and should be accepted even if you are dubious of the appropriateness of such events.

---

Remember that the people you speak with will be rich by local standards, because only the rich, which generally means those with a generous percentage of European heritage, will have the opportunity to negotiate with foreign visitors. You are unlikely to encounter any actual poor people in your client's home, as even the servants are considered rich by the rural poor who inhabit the *campos*. Your client may have a larger house than you do and a good number of servants as well. One or two full-time servants is the norm for middle-class families, as the cost for such services is very low.

## CONVERSATION TOPICS: THE GOOD, THE BAD AND THE UGLY

**What to Talk About**

• **Family—yours and theirs.** This is the all-time optimal never-ending universal topic of Latin American conversation, and it is open to seemingly endless elaborations. Go with it, as it may well be the only topic of conversation you will ever need.

• **Soccer.** Do some research if you are not a fan. The only countries in which soccer will not be a hot conversation topic are Panama and Nicaragua, where baseball and boxing are the topics of choice.

• **American politics.** It is perfectly OK to be proud of the United States and its many accomplishments, but the jingoist ranting of a superpatriot is inappropriate. The United States is not the best place in the world for everyone to live.

• **Food of any type.** Talk about other people's favorite restaurants and the festive dishes they enjoy most at home. You can respond with your favorite dishes. Admire the fact that many in the country have the opportunity to enjoy really fresh food because they have the opportunity to make daily trips to the market.

Tequila or the local moonshine is a good topic if you know about it. If not, ask and people will show you until you slip under the table. See Part Two for more on local dishes in each country.

• **Their country and its landscape.** Latin Americans are very proud of their national identity and accomplishments. Their gross domestic production might be low, but it is growing, and their standard of living is not equal to North America's, but it is improving. They are as emotionally attached to their countries as we are to ours.

• **The price of things.** Do not be surprised if your hosts inquire about prices of items in the United States or about your salary. These are subjects of great curiosity and are good topics of conversation. Be open but do not brag. Act fortunate and humble.

Personal privacy is not a Latin American cultural imperative and is not as highly valued as it is in the United States. My personality permits me to disclose my salary, the value of my house, my weight, my political affiliations, religion and other even more personal information. I have been asked about all of these items at one time or another by relative strangers in Latin America. This can be a bit disconcerting to the uninitiated. Some North Americans are understandably uncomfortable with this type of disclosure; most people find it acceptable to speak openly only about impersonal costs. If you prefer to keep certain information private, more personal questions can usually be dodged with an evasive response and a quick change of topic but such evasion will be noted as a negative for you.

### What Not to Talk About

• **Politics in your host country.** Pretend to know nothing about this topic even if you have read *The CIA World Factbook* on the country and, in fact, have a decent knowledge of local politics. Keep quiet. If your client goes off on the topic, smile and nod your head. When he runs out of steam, change the topic to something neutral. This is one of the "land mine" topics where you do not wish to tread.

*The CIA World Factbook* (www.cia.gov) is a vital source of information for your trip. The section on each country should be read carefully. This information is very unlike the promotional materials you find in guidebooks. It is objective and often actually disliked by the authorities in each country.

• **Any criticism related to the host country.** This would include your hotel, traffic, crowds on the street, poverty, inefficiencies, the local way of life, government, religion or any other conceivable deficiency. If your hosts want to be critical about their country, that is their prerogative, but while they are doing that, you keep quiet and smile. Even if they are obviously correct, do not openly agree with them. Anything you say on the topic, even parroting your host's words, can later be construed as an insensitive remark. Another "land mine" topic.

Do not make any suggestions for improvement in the host country. They know they are underdeveloped and poor. How "Yankee ingenuity" could solve their problems is not an appropriate topic of conversation. Neither is explaining how if only they would copy our system of government, everything would improve.

• **Anything at all related to business.** This is not a topic for discussion outside of the office environment unless the discussion is initiated by your host, which is an extremely unlikely eventuality. Business talk is traditionally not carried out during meals, which are reserved only for relationship building. The atmosphere during these meals is laid back and jovial, usually lubricated with alcohol. The only exception might be at a business breakfast, which is a recent innovation, with a younger Latin American executive who might introduce the novel idea of business-related conversation. Follow his lead.

• **Profanity.** Avoid any profanity that invokes the name of God or Jesus. Even if spoken in an offhanded way, it is considered very offensive. Do not slip on this issue. Avoid any invocation of God or Jesus except when uttered in a most reverential fashion.

This prohibition does not encompass secular obscenities, which are considered macho and are widely utilized in any male social environments. A macho affect is good for you, because it constitutes one of the foundations of the Latin American culture. There is even a special dictionary explaining two hundred variations on the verb *chingar*, or "f—k." There are other milder expletives, such as *caramba*, meaning "good heavens" or "hell," that are acceptable even in mixed company and that will help you seem less a foreigner to your Latin American hosts. Completely avoiding any secular profanity will not help integrate you into the culture, where such language is commonplace.

• **Controversial topics.** If asked your opinion about a controversial topic, give a brief but honest answer and try to move the conversation forward. If asked to explain or defend U.S. policies and culture, economic decisions or immigration reform as they affect the host country, try to keep your answers as short as possible while avoiding spreading inaccurate information. You are there to make friends and do business with them, and not to defend U.S. culture and governmental policies. Stay focused.

• **Excessive criticism of your own country.** If you engage in any serious criticism of the United States, even though your hosts may agree, you will be considered a disloyal citizen for being openly critical of your own country, and therefore not to be trusted. No one wants to do business with someone who calls his president an idiot in front of strangers. Loyalty is valued in Latin America.

• **Anything to do with border fences or illegal immigrants.** This is a sensitive issue, and there is much publicity in the local media about supposed mistreatment of illegal immigrants by the U.S. Border Patrol. As with the other topics to avoid listed in this section, nod, give an empathic statement that does not exacerbate the situation then change the topic.

• **Religion.** Remember that Latin America is up to 90 percent Catholic, so religion is off the conversational menu unless you are Catholic. If you are not Catholic, you aren't going to convert Latin Americans to your religious beliefs, no matter how fervently you believe and express them. Leave the missionary work at home for another day. If you are a practicing Catholic, use it to your advantage to establish a connection by introducing it into the conversation, asking where you can attend services or attend the meeting of a Catholic organization.

• **The Mexican-American War.** Even in the event that you actually know something about the history of this conflict, you are there to do business and not to defend U.S. aggression against your host country.

• **Earthquakes and hurricanes.** These are highly emotional topics for survivors, so avoid them. However, if you personally have survived a serious disaster (e.g., 9/11 or a natural disaster), then the topic establishes a *simpático* affinity circle of disaster survivors to which you belong. Earthquakes large and small are a frequent, if not daily, occurrence in the mountainous regions of Latin America.

## ALCOHOL CONSUMPTION

Alcohol consumption is very common when entertaining in Latin America, which can be challenging if you don't drink or if you're sensitive to alcohol. If you are not a drinker, one option is to say that you are on antibiotics and your doctor has forbidden alcohol, but you would like a soda or any other nonalcoholic beverage. Your hosts will understand this explanation. You might say that alcohol upsets your stomach. If you are recovering from a drinking problem, it would be best not to mention this, as it is still a somewhat foreign concept in the culture. An explanation can be awkward, because it can imply criticism of those who are drinking.

If you do drink alcohol, your clients may drink beyond your capacity to keep up. They may be accustomed to a higher consumption level and the effects of altitude. It is not necessary for you to play macho and keep up with them. Just stop when you choose, leave the drink on the table, and you will be OK. You lose face if you overdo alcohol. Even if everyone else at the table gets absolutely falling-down drunk, you might hear the next day about how drunk the American became.

## Personal Safety Issues

Who will pick you up if you fall down? This is a serious consideration in both a literal and figurative sense. In general, the best policy is to be as risk-averse as possible. Crime is much more common in Latin America than it is in the United States. Normal precautions are in order:

- Whether you are male or female, don't go out by yourself, as there is safety in numbers.
- Leave flashy jewelry in the hotel safe, although leaving it home is the best option.
- Avoid dark streets and depressed neighborhoods. If you have any questions, ask the concierge at your hotel about the neighborhood you will be traveling through. Heed his advice, as he is aware of local conditions, and the characteristics of the various neighborhoods or *colonias* change over time.
- Avoid exploring the neighborhood around the hotel late at night. This is asking for the kind of trouble you don't need. As in any large city in the world, there are likely to be a number of predators lurking in the shadows to take advantage of naive foreigners. If you feel you must go out, consult the concierge first for suggestions.

## GIFT GIVING

Gift giving represents a symbol of friendship and a memento of your meeting. If you are marketing a product, then a small gift is appropriate at each encounter. Keep it modest at the start; in the $25 range is acceptable. A good memento is a coffee-table book of your hometown or state, containing mostly photographs and suitably inscribed by you to your Latin American hosts. Although heavy, books pack easily, are not fragile and to a certain extent are personal.

Gift giving usually escalates as time goes by and the relationship builds. It is not unheard of to inquire at your first *comida* about any item the client or his family might enjoy but which is not currently available in that country. Normally they are quite forthcoming with suggestions, and gifts destined for the hands of their children are particularly welcomed. If you are a buyer, a single small memento at the first meeting is sufficient.

Subsequent visits after you become friends might involve a bottle or two of Chevas, Johnny Walker Black or any other good-quality liquor. These are the preferred libations. Due to high custom duties, this gift will really be considered a nice treat by your middle-class clients, at a very moderate cost to you when purchased at the duty-free shop on the way into the country.

Do not forget your client's secretary on your second visit. Something nice is appropriate. Spend about $20 on perfume in the duty-free shop. If you are a married man, the gift should come "from my wife."

Sharp items, which denote stabbings, and handkerchiefs, which are used at funerals, have a negative connotation. Yellow or orange flowers signify the Day of the Dead. Also do not give gifts made of silver, which your clients already have enough of. Sterling silver .925 is far cheaper in Latin America than in the United States,

and some Latin American silver design shops are definitely high-end. This is an excellent gift to bring home
for friends and family. Ask your host to recommend the
best source, and he or an assistant will probably offer to
accompany you, as it is common practice for local inhabitants to be offered a better price than you would receive
if you were shopping alone.

For large purchases, you may do better with a Latin
American friend, who knows the prices, at hand. He will,
if possible, direct you to a source operated by someone
in his affinity circle, who would naturally offer a good
price to a friend of a friend.

For a more formal gift, typically given upon a contract signing or the like, purchase something in the host
country that is decorative and have it professionally
wrapped. Your administrative assistant will certainly
know where to go for this, and a high-end department
store is a logical choice. A figurine in ceramic or metal,
a really expensively produced globe to represent the
international character of your business, and the like are
good choices. This formal gift is quite important because
it makes everyone aware that you know and respect the
local customs.

The store will not only make suggestions as to what
is appropriate but also send it out to a professional gift
packer, who will overdecorate the item with leaves and
ribbons, etc. Think Easter basket but ten times over. The
wrapping and presentation is as important as the gift.
The professional wrapper will choose the colors and
add-ons that are culturally appropriate and that will
make the best impression. It will be a work of art! The
ensemble is then packed in an open display box and

shrink-wrapped in its entirety, leaving the gift visible to everyone in the room when presented. Make sure your card is inside the shrink-wrap. There is no immediate unwrapping, because it's customary to display the gift for a few days.

It is to be hoped that this gift won't result in a gift back to you the value of which obviously exceeds that of what was given. This is a common type of gift warfare at which you cannot win.

Occasionally such gift-giving competition cannot be avoided. You can simply offer a noncompetitive (i.e., cheaper) gift and give up if that is in your nature. In such instances the client will not feel subsequently challenged by you and the value of his gifts will drop to just a bit more than the gift you presented him. He will consider this a victory and you will spend less money. Alternatively, you may choose to compete. Stupid as it may sound, I compete, but I try to keep the escalation of gift prices at as slow a pace as possible to avoid bankruptcy.

# PART 2

# The Latin American Countries

# INTRODUCTION
# The Countries of
# Latin America

*And remember, no matter where you go, there you are.*
—Earl Mac Rauch

The Latin American culture is regional in scope, yet there are some differences evident in each of these seventeen countries. None of these cultural quirks alters the basic mind-set of the culture, but they constitute useful and interesting variations on the basic themes of relationships, corruption and procrastination, of which you should be aware while traveling in these countries. All except Chile, Uruguay and Costa Rica are to some extent endemically corrupt in the Latin American tradition. None of them effectively enforces trademark or copyright laws.

The best and most fascinating information about these countries can be obtained from *The CIA World Factbook* (www.cia.gov). Profiles are given, in superb detail, for every nation in the world and should be required reading for even the most experienced traveler.

There are two types of warnings issued by the U.S. government: one by the CIA, the other by the State Department. *The CIA World Factbook* gives excerpted travel warnings from either the CIA or the State Department when appropriate, in the country profiles where specific conditions warrant attention. For example, two countries, Bolivia and Colombia, have earned State Department Travel Alerts, which strongly suggest that they be avoided by potential visitors. The State Department has pulled all nonessential personnel from these countries.

The profiles that follow include a brief description of each of the Latin American countries and an explanation of the local customs and culture, along with some warnings. Information on the following topics is also provided for each country:

- **The population**, rounded to the nearest million
- **Capital city**
- **The Gross Domestic Product (GDP)** per person is indicated, which in the United States is $46,000 per person. This amount gives you an approximate idea of relative prosperity. Many Mesoamerican countries have a GDP of around $4,000, which indicates that the people earn less than a tenth of what an average North American earns. You can conclude that these countries don't have much money to spend on anything you might be offering.
- **The geographic size** of each country is given in square kilometers. Note that the United States encompasses 9,826,630 square kilometers. I also give you a cross-reference, which compares each country's size to a location in the United States. This cross-reference is perhaps more useful to you than

size expressed in square kilometers, as it permits you to visualize the country relative to a known factor.

- **The health risk indicator** as indicated in *The CIA World Factbook*, ranging from normal, which would be characteristic of the United States and Western Europe, to intermediate, high and then on to very high. According to the CIA, "the degree of risk is assessed by considering the foreign nature of these infectious diseases, their severity, and the probability of being affected by the diseases present." The specific warnings for each country are included in each country's profile. As a general consideration, make sure your tetanus shot is current regardless of where you travel.
- **Contact information**, consisting of telephone area codes with dialing instructions and Internet extensions.
- **Visa information.** Most Latin American countries will grant a tourist visa upon your arrival. However, for those who require previous approval for a visa, a word of advice. You can handle the matter with the appropriate consulate on your own before you leave. There are also commercial services advertising on the Internet that can take care of this matter for a fee over and above the fee for the visa itself. Why utilize these services? Your individual submission may not be returned to you in a timely fashion when submitted directly, either because you have made an error on the documentation, which is complex, have forgotten a piece of paper or a signature, or the characteristic procrastination evident in Latin American culture has come into play. Some

of the largest providers are www.visahq.com, www
.visalatam.com and www.abriggs.com.

- **The volume and percentages of trade** going to and
coming from the United States are indicated for each
country. This is crucial information. For example,
statistically Ecuador essentially does no business
with the United States either as an importer or as an
exporter. When looking at these percentages, you
must take into consideration the volume of trade.
Five percent of $100 billion has more potential for
you than 50 percent of $50 million.

- **The exchange rates** indicated are approximate at
the time of this publication but should be verified
again in *The CIA World Factbook* (www.cia.gov) prior
to departure.

- **About the Country** is a short description of the
social and political conditions in each Latin American country.

- There is reference to **specialized food** items you
may encounter when visiting with your clients, as
well as **local customs**.

- Relevant warnings concerning **personal safety**
are provided, based on information from the State
Department and the CIA.

- **Information on U.S. diplomatic representatives**
in each country and their corresponding representatives in Washington, DC, as well as the countries'
various consulates in the United States, is provided.
The proper names of the ambassadors are given. It
is unlikely that you will ever actually speak with an
ambassador, but rather you will be directed to some
commercial attaché, which is fine for your purposes.

Three very small countries in South America are not included on the list. Guiana, which is English; Surinam, which is Dutch; and French Guiana, which is, unsurprisingly, French. None of these countries are considered Latin American in character.

# ARGENTINA

**Basic Information**

> Population: 40 million
> Capital City: Buenos Aires
> GDP: $13,000 per person
> Size: 2,766,890 sq km, which is equal to 3/10 of the United States
> Health Risk: intermediate

**Contact Information**

> Telephone: 011 54 + city code + telephone number
> Internet Extension: .ar

**Visa Information**

U.S. citizens don't need a visa for visits of up to ninety days, for tourism or business. No inoculations are required.

**Trade**

- **Imports:** machinery, motor vehicles, petroleum and natural gas, organic chemicals and plastics. Only 12 percent of Argentina imports come from the United States.
- **Exports:** soybeans, petroleum and gas, vehicles, corn and wheat. Only 9 percent of Argentinean exports are sent to the United States.
- **Exchange Rate:** 3 Argentine pesos per U.S. dollar

## About the Country

Argentina is the land of the tango and, after Brazil, the second-largest country in Latin America. Both Americans and American goods are warmly welcomed here. Argentina, along with Mexico, Brazil, Chile, Costa Rica and Uruguay, is one of the strongest economic markets in Latin America, which will probably be the focus of your commercial interest.

Buenos Aires, known as the Paris of Latin America, is the capital and the center of all things Argentinean. It is one of the most formal cities in Latin America. The clothing styles worn by the business class are up-to-the-minute French fashion.

Argentina is a reasonably safe country, by Latin American standards, for the 300,000 U.S. visitors each year. There has been a strong recovery after the 2001 economic depression. More than 450 U.S. companies are currently operating in Argentina and employ more than 150,000 Argentine workers.

Argentineans are enthusiastic about soccer and are among the world's best polo players. Their love of horses is best exemplified by the iconic image of the Argentine *gaucho* in his *serape*, riding across the seemingly endless *pampas*.

## Things to Remember
### LOCAL CUSTOMS

- Their winter is our summer, so it is unproductive to travel and conduct business meetings in Argentina during January and February, since most businesses are closed or working on a limited schedule. Businesspeople with children out of school take vacation, so availability is problematical. April through November are the best months for business travel to Argentina.

- Argentineans are louder and more animated in their conversations than other Latin Americans. The social dynamic is like a large animated family gathering, but meetings are considered serious business. Do not be aggressive.

- A sweeping gesture beginning under the chin and continuing up over the top of the head is used to indicate, "I don't know" or "I don't care."

- Touching together the thumb and index finger and tapping them with the other index finger indicates "Hurry up" or "a lot."

- Maintain somewhat more eye contact here than in other Latin American countries. Hand gestures should be minimized.

**FOOD**

This is a meat-based cuisine, so you should experience few dietary difficulties unless you are a vegetarian. The sauces are generally not very *picante*. If you come across something that you believe you won't like, try it and you may well be surprised. As in other Latin American countries, refusing a gift of food is equivalent to refusing the person offering it and is therefore considered rude.

Argentina does not have an obvious traditional cuisine outside of the omnipresence of beef. Many immigrant groups have over the centuries contributed the best from their native cuisine to this melting pot. Beef may be served at every meal. Barbecue is important. Traditionally, the whole animal is roasted over a pit. Most dinners start at eight or nine and may well run to midnight.

The national drink is maté, brewed from yerba maté, a bush related to the holly, and is commonly drunk throughout the southern part of the continent. Consumed on just about every occasion, through long silver straws from a common container, maté tastes exactly like a caffeinated herbal tea. There is usually some ritual performed around its presentation. Don't refuse.

**WARNINGS**

- **State Department warning:** "Traffic accidents are the primary threat to life and limb in Argentina. Pedestrians and drivers should exercise caution. Drivers frequently ignore traffic laws and vehicles often travel at excessive speeds. The rate and toll of traffic accidents has been a topic of much media attention. The Institute of Road Safety and Education, a private Buenos Aires organization dedicated to transportation safety issues, reports that Argentina has the highest traffic mortality rate in South America per 100,000 inhabitants." More on this topic can be found at http://travel.state.gov/travel.

- Pickpockets are in abundance, utilizing a plethora of scams. One of the more unconventional schemes involves spraying you with some mustard. A concerned citizen rushes forward to help you clean up the mess and in the resulting confusion, his or her confederate picks your pocket.

- There are some hit-and-run kidnappings, which usually don't result in physical harm. In this instance, an adult is forcibly escorted to the nearest ATM, where the maximum withdrawal is added to what the victim has in his pockets and stolen. The victim is then released.
- Bad conversation topics are the Perón era and the conflict in the Falkland Islands, which the Argentineans refer to as the Malvinas Islands and in which the United States sided with the "wrong" country as far as they are concerned.

## Argentinean Diplomatic Representation in the United States

Ambassador Héctor Marcos Timerman
1600 New Hampshire Avenue NW
Washington, DC 20009
Telephone: (202) 238-6400

## Consulates General

Atlanta, Chicago, Houston, Los Angeles, Miami and New York

## U.S. Diplomatic Representation in Argentina

Ambassador Earl Anthony Wayne
Avenida Colombia 4300
C1425GMN Buenos Aires, Argentina
Telephone: 011-54-11-5777-4533
www.embassyofargentina.us

# BOLIVIA

## Basic Information

Population: 9 million

Capital City: La Paz (administrative) and Sucre (legislative)

GDP: $4,000

Size: 1,098,580 sq km, three times the size of Montana

Health Risk: high

## Contact Information

Telephone: 011-591 + city code + telephone number

Internet Extension: .bo

## Visa Information

A visa and yellow fever vaccination certificate are required before travel. The visa can be secured by you or by agents employed on your behalf providing the Bolivian consulate with:

- A completed, sworn and notarized statement for visa application, with an additional passport-size photograph
- A copy of your current American passport with at least six months validity
- A copy of the hotel reservation or the invitation letter from Bolivian friends or relatives, indicating the host address
- A copy of your round-trip ticket and a bank statement that shows economic solvency, or a copy of a credit card

- A copy of your yellow fever vaccination certificate. A single dose confers immunity lasting ten years or more. This vaccine is only administered at designated yellow fever vaccination centers. The locations of these sites can be provided by your local health department. For more information, visit www.cdc.gov/travel/yellowBookCh4.
- A visa fee of $100

For additional information on Bolivia's visa requirements, visit www.bolivia-usa.org/consulares.

**Trade**
- **Imports:** petroleum products, plastics, paper, aircraft and aircraft parts, prepared foods, automobiles, insecticides and soybeans. About 10 percent of Bolivian imports come from the United States.
- **Exports:** natural gas, soybeans, crude petroleum, zinc ore and tin. About 10 percent of Bolivian exports are sent to the United States.
- **Exchange Rate:** 8 bolivianos per U.S. dollar

**About the Country**
Bolivia is a country of extremes. It is one of the poorest countries in the world and is the highest and most isolated country in South America. Among South American countries, Bolivia has the largest proportion (60 percent) of indigenous people who maintain their traditional values and beliefs.

The seasons are reversed, so December through February are their summer months, and the rainy season. Moving about becomes problematic during this period, and many streets are impassable. It is not a good time to visit Bolivia.

Though rich in mineral and energy resources, Bolivia is the second-poorest South American country. Along with Paraguay, the poorest country on the continent, it is one of two landlocked nations in South America. Wealthy urban elites, mostly of Spanish ancestry, traditionally dominate political and economic life there. The vast majority of Bolivians are low-income subsistence farmers, miners, small traders or artisans. In terms of topography, isolation, altitude, treatment of indigenous population and poverty, Bolivia is unfavorably compared to Tibet.

Bolivia generally welcomes foreign investment; nevertheless, it is a difficult place to do business. Social unrest, arbitrary regulatory decisions, widespread corruption and a disabling bureaucracy make doing business unappealing to foreigners. Coupled with double-digit inflation and government social policies, which have exacerbated racial and economic tensions between the indigenous populations in the western part of the country and the more Spanish communities in the east, these conditions have not encouraged prosperity and, in fact, the ongoing conflict is a recipe for disaster.

Drugs remain a problem for Bolivia, the world's third-largest cultivator of coca, after Colombia and Peru. Criminal law procedures are famously bizarre. Arrests are more or less arbitrary. You are guilty until you can prove to the police that you are innocent, and you remain in jail under inhumane conditions until you do so. No bail. No parole. No habeas corpus. Since no one is in a particular hurry, it can take weeks, even months, for you to appear before a corrupt judge. While jailed, you must pay bribes for room and board that can come to $5,000 a week for basic livable accommodations.

## Things to Remember
### LOCAL CUSTOMS

- When shaking hands, keep eye contact and tilt your head as if making a slight bow.
- Let your client set the conversational agenda. Bolivians are a quiet and sober people, which is a general characteristic of countries with a Mayan indigenous population, as opposed to individuals identified with the more effusive Spanish culture. Do not talk about your family or other personal matters until your host brings up the subject.
- Nepotism is a common practice throughout Latin America, even if the person's qualifications are nonexistent. It is one of the reasons that the local economies do not function beyond the basic minimums necessary for life. The practice is especially prevalent in Bolivia.

### FOOD

The ubiquitous potato in several different guises is an important element at every meal in Bolivia. Due to the dire poverty, restaurants are a luxury and street stalls out of reach for many. Follow the locals. If the street stall is crowded, the food is probably good. The meat in most restaurants is unidentifiable, particularly in the stews. Among the dishes on the Bolivian menu are:

- *Ají de lengua:* spicy cow tongue
- *Cuy:* roasted guinea pig (see page 206 for a complete description of this famous dish)

- *Fricasé:* spicy pork meat stew
- *Fritanga:* spicy pork and egg stew
- *Majao:* rice and meat dish
- *Picante de pollo:* spicy chicken
- *Saisi:* spicy meat
- *Salteñas:* meat or chicken turnovers
- *Charque de llama:* dried llama meat, fried, served with stewed corn, hard-cooked eggs and cheese
- The local moonshine is called *chicha*, which is a homemade concoction brewed from fermented corn. It is known to have been the sacred drink of the Incas.

**WARNINGS**

- Bolivian culture is essentially a do-as-little-as-possible environment. Minimal productivity is expected from the populace. Efficiency is neither demanded nor rewarded. Deadlines are not taken seriously. There is an "If I don't do it today, then perhaps I won't have to do it tomorrow" philosophy.
- Americans are not very popular in Bolivia, and many citizens blame the nation's poverty on the United States.
- Telephone service is erratic and perhaps the worst in Latin America, although it is slowly improving as the system is modernized. There are frequent disconnects, and line noise is the norm, although voice communication is usually audible. Telephones are located in the larger cities. Out in the countryside there may be no service at all.
- Women are victims of blatant sexual harassment in the chauvinistic society, although this practice

is against Bolivian law. It is not to your advantage to point this out to your client, but keep your self-respect by neither smiling at nor participating in the "fun."

- Women should be aware that eye contact, for more than a few seconds, might be interpreted as a suggestion for a dalliance. Should you ever accept such an invitation without a duenna present, bring your pepper spray, because you will probably need it.

## Bolivian Diplomatic Representation in the United States

Ambassador (vacant); Chargé d'Affaires Erika Dueñas
3014 Massachusetts Avenue NW
Washington, DC 20008
Telephone: (202) 483-4410

## Consulates General

Houston, Los Angeles, Miami, New York, Oklahoma City, San Francisco, Seattle and Washington, DC

## U.S. Diplomatic Representation in Bolivia

Ambassador (vacant); Chargé d'Affaires Krishna Urs
Avenida Arce 2780, Casilla 425
La Paz, Bolivia
Telephone: 011-591-2-216-8000
http://bolivia.usembassy.gov

# BRAZIL

## Basic Information

Population: 190 million
Capital City: Brasília

GDP: $10,000

Size: 8,511,965 sq km, which is slightly smaller than the United States

Health Risk: unrated (see below)

## Contact Information

Telephone: 011-55 + city code + telephone number

Internet Extension: .br

## Visa Information

A yellow fever inoculation is strongly recommended for all visitors, which must be received at least two weeks before leaving for Brazil.

In the majority of Latin American countries a tourist visa can be obtained at the airport upon debarking from your airplane. No prior approval is necessary. For most business visas there is prior approval required, encompassing some paperwork. None of this is so in Brazil. Nothing comes close in paperwork complexity to Brazil, for either a business or a tourist visa.

To receive a tourist visa, you or a company employed on your behalf will need to bring to a Brazilian consulate the following items:

- Your passport, valid for at least six months after your arrival date in Brazil
- A visa application form filled out on both sides and signed
- One recent two-by-two passport photo, front view with white background
- Your round-trip ticket

- The consulate may request additional documentation as deemed necessary.
- $130 U.S. postal money order made out to the Brazilian consulate. No other form of payment will be accepted.

To receive a business visa, you will require all of the above plus a quantity of other documents, which must be officially translated and notarized. Consult the consulate for the latest version of this list. This is a major paperwork project, which will require several weeks to complete.

**Trade**
- **Imports:** machinery, electrical and transport equipment, chemical products, oil, automotive parts and electronics. Approximately 16 percent of the imports are from the United States.
- **Exports:** transport equipment, iron ore, soybeans, footwear, coffee and autos. Approximately 18 percent of exports are to the United States.
- **Exchange Rate:** 2 Brazilian reals per U.S. dollar

**About the Country**
The largest country in South America in terms of both population and area, Brazil shares common boundaries with every South American country except Chile and Ecuador. Along with Argentina, Chile, Uruguay and Mexico, Brazil is one of the best places to do business in Latin America. The country is an extremely large market, and the dollar remains relatively strong against the

real, making your merchandise relatively less expensive. It is also one of the largest democracies in the world. The people are famously friendly.

The Brazilian customs procedures are an infamous nightmare in which combined duties and fees equaling more than the original value of the merchandise can be paid by you or your client. These duties drive up the prices Brazilians pay for your North American merchandise. The legal system is weak and corrupt, and there are essentially no intellectual property rights enforced.

Brazil is the only Portuguese-speaking country in Latin America. More than half the population identify themselves as being of European descent. It is a rich country. Like Mexico, it has good land, abundant natural resources and a strong industrial sector, centered around São Paulo. With a seemingly endless abundance of sugar, the country's potential for rapid growth in the manufacture of ethyl alcohol for fuel is obvious.

Class distinctions can be harsh in both the cities and rural areas of Brazil. Most of the vast rain forests are owned by a very few incredibly wealthy families. Approximately a third of the population of Rio de Janeiro lives in truly horrible *favelas*, or slums.

This is a very young society, with 50 percent of the population being under twenty years of age. Most people on the street look as if they just came off a magazine cover. In Rio, grandmothers push grandchildren around supermarkets while dressed in their bikinis. Plastic surgeons are not in short supply.

Rio de Janeiro is justifiably famous, but very little business is actually transacted in the city, except in the banking and insurance sectors. There is no industry in the area. The emphasis is on tourism and having a fantastic time on the beaches and in the clubs. All of the government offices are out in the jungle in Brasília, which is the capital of Brazil, but there is not much else out there.

The center of manufacturing and industry is São Paulo, which is the largest city in Latin America and one of the largest in the world. It is about an hour by air from Rio. São Paulo is primarily a manufacturing city, with the air pollution and other problems that accompany industry. Interestingly, São Paulo has the largest urban Japanese population found outside of Japan.

Mardi Gras in Rio de Janeiro is the seminal event in the Brazilian year, and it should be experienced at least once in everyone's lifetime. There is nothing on earth like this celebration, and no words or photographs can begin to do it justice. The energy is fantastic. In comparison, it makes the New Orleans Mardi Gras seem as sedate as a church picnic. No business is conducted during the two weeks before and a few days after (for recuperation and cleanup) this event, which occurs around late February, during the weeks before Ash Wednesday. It is very hot at this time of year, so little, if any, apparel is required.

## Things to Remember
### LOCAL CUSTOMS

- Having a Portuguese-language business card is an important social nicety in Brazil and demonstrates that you are not an in-and-out, never-to-be-seen-again executive. Within twenty-four hours, you can have your business cards translated and printed. Ask your hotel to recommend a nearby printer.

- When you meet someone for the first time, you should shake hands. A common term used is *muito prazer*, or my pleasure.
- Eye contact, but not staring, is important as a demonstration of sincerity and interest in both the conversation and the person speaking.
- Due to the extremely high duty rate on imported merchandise, small electronic items, although locally available in Brazil, are often appreciated as gifts. Good choices include the latest high-quality scientific calculators, electronic address books and day-timers, pocket CD and mp3 players, and radios. They are not fragile and are easy to pack.
- To express appreciation, a Brazilian may appear to pinch his earlobe between thumb and forefinger.
- Flicking the fingertips underneath the chin indicates that you don't know the answer to a question.
- Do not be upset if personal questions are asked. Although Brazilians are reticent about their own personal lives, they may nevertheless ask seemingly intrusive questions about your children, income, religion and marital status. Answer as politely as you can.
- Men making comments or whistling at passing women is part of the local culture. While this is often the norm, do not participate.

**FOOD**

Brazilians eat very late. Many of the better restaurants do not open until 8 p.m. and people arrive around 9 p.m. Dinner parties often continue until 2 a.m., and sometimes later.

Some interesting specialties you will encounter while in Brazil include:

- *Feijoada*, one of the country's two signature dishes. This is a black bean and pork dish that comes with rice and kale.
- *Churrasco*, the second famous dish, is a barbecue quite unlike anything you will experience outside an authentic Brazilian restaurant. Waiters walk around the dining room with skewers holding large chunks of meat. There might be twelve varieties of meat circulating. The waiter puts the end of the skewer on your plate and slices off meat until you tell him to stop. Then along comes the next waiter with another cut of meat. Same drill.
- *Caipirinha* is the local moonshine of choice and is made from cane alcohol, lime slices, ice and sugar, which are muddled with a wooden mortar in your old-fashioned glass.

### WARNINGS

- Brazil's murder rate is more than four times higher than that of the United States. Rates for other crimes are similarly high. The majority of crimes are not solved.
- Street crime remains a problem for visitors and local residents alike, especially in the evenings and late at night. Foreign tourists are often targets of crime, and Americans are not exempt. This targeting occurs in all tourist areas but is especially problematic in Rio de Janeiro, Salvador and Recife.
- Bad conversation topics include Argentina, with which Brazil has a long-term animosity. Politics,

poverty, the destruction of the rain forest, street kids, crime and corruption should also be avoided. Most Brazilians suffer from these plagues, and feel powerless to change their social situation. They really don't want to talk to you about these issues.

- Never leave as soon as an open-ended meeting is over, and all meetings are essentially open-ended. This action will insult your colleagues and leave them with the impression that you believe that you have more important things to do than spend time with them. For this reason, if the meeting is important to you, don't make other appointments for that day.

- Beware of good Samaritans who offer to help you, as they may have an ulterior motive.

- Check your credit card balance online frequently to make sure there are no unauthorized charges.

## Brazilian Representation in the United States

Ambassador Antonio de Aguiar Patriota
3006 Massachusetts Avenue NW
Washington, DC 20008
Telephone: (202) 238-2700

## Consulates General

Boston, Chicago, Houston, Los Angeles, Miami, New York and San Francisco
www.brasilemb.org

## U.S. Representatives in Brazil

Ambassador Clifford M. Sobel
Avenida das Nações, Quadra 801, Lote 3

Distrito Federal Cep 70403-900, Brasília
Telephone: 011-55-61-3312-7000

## Consulates General
Rio de Janeiro, Sao Paulo and Recife

# CHILE

## Basic Information
Population: 16 million
Capital City: Santiago
Size: 756,950 sq km, which is about twice the size of
    Montana
GDP: $14,000
Health Risk: normal

## Contact Information
Telephone: 011-54 + city code + telephone number
Internet Extension: .cl

## Visa Information
Tourist visas may be obtained at the airport on arrival
for a fee of $100. Check with the Chilean consulate for
current requirements for business visas.

## Trade
- **Imports:** petroleum, chemicals, electrical and tele-
  communications equipment, industrial machinery,
  vehicles and natural gas. Approximately 16 percent
  of Chilean imports are from the United States.

- **Exports:** copper, fruit, fish products, paper and
  pulp, chemicals and wine. Approximately 15 percent of Chilean exports are to the United States.
- **Exchange Rate:** 525 Chilean pesos per U.S. dollar

## About the Country

Chile is a country with attractions ranging from the vol-
canic peaks of the Andes to the forests of the Lake District.
It is the world's longest country from north to south and
stretches more than 2,700 miles along the southwestern
coast of South America. This distance is roughly the same
as that from San Francisco to New York. At the same time,
its width never exceeds 150 miles, making the country
more than eighteen times longer than at its widest point.

Chile is one of South America's most stable and pros-
perous nations and has been relatively free of the coups
and arbitrary government regulations that have blighted
much of Latin America. It is also the least corrupt nation
in Latin America and provides a safe haven for business development. Laws are consistent and equitably
enforced. Chileans speak the best classical Spanish in
Latin America, and English is spoken by many of the
well-educated businesspeople.

This is a small and competitive market. There is no
customs duty on trade with the United States either for
imports or for exports.

About one-third of the population lives in Santiago,
which is the capital. Chileans are viewed as hard workers
in comparison to their Latin American neighbors. There
is a noticeable difference between the upper and lower
classes, and the two never mix socially. But no social
unrest is currently evident.

Chileans are justifiably proud of their famous white wine, which is competitive with the best vintages around the world.

## Things to Remember
### LOCAL CUSTOMS

- Do not wear anything on your lapel, as this is considered some sort of advertisement or political statement and unbecoming of a sophisticated person.
- Old-fashioned common courtesy is still much in fashion. When a woman enters the room, the men all stand. If a woman offers her hand, shake it. If her hands remain at her sides, do nothing but smile at her.
- Maintaining eye contact more than is the norm in Latin America is necessary to show interest.
- Punctuality is respected in Chile. Meetings start promptly, and an ending time for the meeting is usually established in advance.
- Dramatic gestures are part of customary conversation and are normal when you wish to convince someone of the veracity of your position.
- A good conversation gambit is Easter Island, administered by Chile as a national park. It is famous both for its remoteness (about fifteen hundred miles off the coast of Chile) and for the enormous stone heads of mysterious origin residing there. A three-day detour to Easter Island is a worthwhile journey if time permits.

### FOOD

The food of Chile is quite bland, if not boring, compared to the rest of the Latin American countries. The menus consist of standard Latin American fare but without much exceptional flavor. Contrary to the similarities in the nomenclature, the chili is not part of the culinary repertoire in Chile.

- *Pisco*, the local moonshine, is alcohol distilled from grapes, of which Chile has an abundance. Naturally, the wine is fabulous.
- A fun drink called *bigoteado* contains the combined leftovers from any glasses that happen to be lying around. It naturally tastes awful, and it is usually given as a joke when the recipient is so drunk he doesn't know what he is drinking. If you let yourself get that intoxicated, you deserve two *bigoteados* and a whole bottle of aspirin.

**WARNINGS**
- Unlike people of other Latin American countries, Chileans don't bargain in stores or street markets. It is illegal in Chile to sell something and not issue an official invoice, thus keeping businesses honest and taxes paid.
- Bad conversation topics include human rights and events in recent Chilean history involving the armed forces. These are highly emotional and divisive issues among Chileans.
- Don't serve wine with your left hand as this is seen as disrespectful, even if you are left-handed. Wines, especially white wines, hold a special place of honor in Chile and deserve respect.
- Holding the palm upward and then spreading the fingers signals that someone is not very intelligent, or worse.

- Slapping your right fist into your left open palm is considered obscene and perhaps an indication of the intent of physical aggression.
- Raising your right fist to head level is a common greeting between Communist Party members, and unless you happen to be a true believer or have downed two *bigoteados*, I suggest that you forgo the gesture.

## Chilean Representation in the United States

Ambassador Mariano Fernández Amunátegui
1732 Massachusetts Avenue NW
Washington, DC 20036
Telephone: (202) 785-1746
embassy@embassyofchile.org

## Consulates General

Chicago, Houston, Los Angeles, Miami, New York, Philadelphia, San Francisco and San Juan

## U.S. Representation in Chile

Ambassador Paul E. Simons
Avenida Andrés Bello 2800, Las Condes
Santiago, Chile
Telephone: 011-56-2-232-2600

# COLOMBIA

## Basic Information

Population: 44 million
Capital City: Bogotá (Santa Fe de Bogotá)
Size: 1,138,910 sq km, or about twice the size of Texas

GDP: $7,000
Health Risk: high

## Contact Information
Telephone: 011-57 + city code + telephone number
Internet extension: .co

## Visa Information
Both tourist and business visas can be obtained on arrival at the airport.

## Trade
- **Imports:** industrial equipment, transportation equipment, consumer goods, chemicals, paper products, fuels and electricity. Approximately 26 percent of Colombian imports are from the United States.
- **Exports:** petroleum, coffee, coal, nickel, emeralds, apparel, bananas and cut flowers. Approximately 35 percent of Colombian exports are to the United States.
- **Exchange Rate:** 2 Colombian pesos per U.S. dollar

## About the Country
Colombia has substantial and varied natural resources, including oil reserves, and is a major producer of gold, silver, emeralds, platinum, coal and cocaine. The country's diverse culture reflects the indigenous, Spanish and African origins of its people. It is the fourth-largest country in Latin America and one of the continent's most populous nations.

Colombia has been ravaged by a decades-long violent conflict involving outlawed armed groups, drug cartels and the concomitant gross violations of human rights. Some 300,000 people have fled the country.

The country is enjoying a measure of prosperity in spite of fairly constant armed conflict and the implementation of austere government budgeting. The reduction of public debt and strategies for export-oriented growth have been beneficial, while improvement in domestic security and high commodity prices for oil and cocaine exports are creating a growth economy with low inflation.

Unfortunately, the country is best known for its drug trade and violence and is a major illicit producer of coca, opium poppy and cannabis. In fact, it has the distinction of being the world's largest producer of coca derivatives, and supplies cocaine to most of the U.S. market as well as to the great remainder of the international drug market. It is illegal under U.S. law for Americans to do business with anyone even remotely connected to the drug trade.

On the positive side, if you can consider trade of this type to have a positive side, the influx of drug money has encouraged a growing middle class. Contravening this impetus to grow, there are extremely high rates of duty on imported goods and restrictive trade laws, which are a great detriment to normal business development.

Colombia is characterized by an unstable social and business environment. In a country of small and undercapitalized family-owned companies, businesses tend to lack the long-term perspective of larger corporations. It has been their experience that planning is often futile, and future business prospects are therefore unattended to in favor of what can be gained in the immediate future.

The society is characterized by distinct social differences, a combination of family origin, education and income level. Drug lords have high incomes, but that does not guarantee access to the upper social circles. However, low income will guarantee social isolation.

## Things to Remember
### LOCAL CUSTOMS

- Formality increases as you move inland.
- Colombians more than most other Latin Americans are punctual within the business environment.
- It is common to stand close together in the Latin American fashion; however, there is less physical contact during conversation in Colombia than in other Latin American countries.
- The best conversation topic is family (yours and theirs). The history and culture of our respective nations provides for interesting conversation also, as does coffee, which is the national passion.
- Colombian women will often substitute the gesture of holding your forearms for a handshake in both a business and social setting.

### FOOD

Colombian food is a rather plain mixture of European and local ingredients. Among the popular dishes are:

- *Bandeja paisa*, or the "national flag," is a favorite consisting of white rice, red beans, ground beef, plantain, dirty rice with chorizo, dried pork skins, arepa, avocado and a fried egg. The colors are meant to bear a fanciful relationship to the Colombian flag. It is not a light snack.

- *Ajiaco* is the other national favorite and is a type of soup with chicken on the bone, large chunks of corn on the cob, two or three kinds of native potatoes and *guasca*, a weedy, aromatic herb common in all Latin America, which tastes like oregano.

- *Sancocho* is a soup combining vegetables and poultry or fish, which usually contains yucca and maize and is frequently eaten with banana slices.

- *Cuchuco* is a thick soup made of wheat, broad beans, potatoes, ribs and peas.

- The local moonshine is called *chicha*. It can be prepared from virtually anything, but is typically made from corn.

**WARNINGS**
- According to the CIA, drug-related crime has become the most common cause of death in Colombia after cancer. Together with the political violence, this has made Colombia one of the most violent countries in the world, deterring investors and tourists alike. A complete text of the State Department warning can be found at http://travel.state.gov/travel/cis_pa_tw/cis_pa_tw_1168.html.

- Avoid any discussion of the drug traffic problem and the stereotypes associated with it. Only a minuscule proportion of the population is directly involved in the drug trafficking per se, although many in the middle

class profit indirectly from the business. The majority
of Colombians are understandably very sensitive to
being labeled with the sobriquet of drug trafficker.

- Two pointing index fingers held apart is an obscene
  gesture in Colombia.
- Colombians indicate that someone is stingy by tapping their fingers on their elbow.
- Female executives should be especially sensitive about
  doing anything that might be considered flirtatious.
  Be very careful and remember where you are—all the
  macho charm floating about notwithstanding. Complaints to the police after the fact provide no redress
  and may well result in further sexual abuse.

## Colombian Diplomatic Representation
## in United States

Ambassador Carolina Barco Isakson
2118 Leroy Place NW
Washington, DC 20008
Telephone: (202) 387-8338

## Consulates General

Atlanta; Boston; Chicago; Houston; Los Angeles; Miami;
New York; San Francisco; San Juan, Puerto Rico; and
Washington, DC
www.colombiaemb.org

## U.S. Diplomatic Representation in Colombia

Ambassador William R. Brownfield
Calle 24 Bis No. 48–50
Bogotá, Colombia
Telephone: 011-57-1-315-0811

# COSTA RICA

**Basic Information**

Population: 4 million

Capital City: San José

GDP: $14,000

Size: 51,100 sq km, which is slightly smaller than West Virginia

Health Risk: intermediate

**Contact Information**

Telephone: 011 + 506 + telephone number

Internet Extension: .cr

**Visa Information**

No visa is required for either tourists or businesspeople. A visitor's card will be issued upon arrival at the airport. You must have a yellow fever certificate if you are entering Costa Rica from Bolivia, Brazil, Colombia, Ecuador, Peru or Venezuela.

**Trade**

- **Imports:** raw materials, consumer goods, capital equipment, petroleum and construction materials. About 41 percent of their imports are from the United States.
- **Exports:** bananas, pineapples, coffee, melons, ornamental plants, sugar, seafood, electronic components and medical equipment. About 27 percent of their exports are to the United States.
- **Exchange Rate:** 520 Costa Rican colones per U.S. dollar

**About the Country**

Costa Rica in many respects is a major exception to the rules and practices that govern Latin American culture and which so vex American businesspeople. It is one of the most stable countries in Latin America. The people have elected to forgo an army, which is an institution that has been the source of problems for so many other Latin Americans. Costa Ricans, who call themselves Ticos, have one of the highest living standards in our hemisphere. There is a well-developed social welfare system, and social unrest is unheard of, as are guerrillas, urban or otherwise. Land ownership is widespread. More than 95 percent of the people are of European descent. Although a very small country in terms of population and area, Costa Rica is a very pleasant society in which to live and do business.

In a reversal of the normal process, Costa Rican voters narrowly approved a free trade deal with the United States in 2007. Other Latin American countries would jump at the opportunity, as the United States has been quite selective in choosing the countries for partnership in free trade arrangements.

The country's industrial base is small, but Costa Rica has expanded its economy to include strong technology and tourism industries. Costa Rica has become synonymous with the term "ecotourism," and naturalists can find 1,000 species of orchids and 850 species of birds in this virtually unspoiled and beautiful nation.

There is a large community of English-speaking expatriates living in Costa Rica who are very popular with Costa Ricans, and English has effectively become a second language. Costa Rica's is a fiercely democratic culture, with a belief in peace through negotiations. The country is about as far from the Latin American norm as you can get.

Costa Rica has the highest number of lawyers per capita than any other country in Mesoamerica.

### Things to Remember
#### LOCAL CUSTOMS

- Ticos are an optimistic and friendly people and very open to outsiders. Their ways of thinking are remarkably similar to those in the United States, therefore the businessperson feels "at home" in a way that is not possible in other Latin American countries.
- Costa Rica is the only country in Latin America where any type of politics is always a topic for lively and informative conversation. The political outlook is very much like it is in the United States, and you can openly say what you believe to be true.
- Costa Rican businesspeople are the most punctual in Latin America. Meetings start on time, and lunch is a brief affair lasting no more than an hour. Ticos are even more formal than most other Latin Americans, with jackets and ties habitually worn during business hours.
- Contrary to Latin American cultural norms, business entertaining in Costa Rica takes place in the evening, over a dinner, which starts and ends at a reasonable hour so that everyone can get to work the next morning.

**FOOD**

Costa Rican fare follows the generic Latin American food model with few distinguishing characteristics. Some popular dishes include:

- *Gallo pinto:* the national dish of fried rice and black beans
- *Casado:* a ubiquitous dish containing a wide variety of foods, such as chicken, rice, beans, plantains and cheese, on one plate. It changes from day to day and restaurant to restaurant. It is like the mythical "blue plate special" in the United States and is an inexpensive fixed-price option.
- Turtle eggs are a very popular dish in many bars, but they are an acquired taste.
- *Arroz guacho:* sticky rice
- *Hígado en salsa:* beef liver with salsa
- *Barbudos:* a string bean omelet
- *Mondongo:* beef stomach soup
- The local moonshine is called *guaro* and is a very alcoholic clear spirit distilled from sugarcane. In the more rural areas you might find *vino de coyol*, which is a drink distilled from liquid that is collected from holes in the trunk of a *coyol*, which is a very spiny palm.

**WARNINGS**

- A lot of gesturing, which is so common in other parts of Latin America, is considered inappropriate in Costa Rica. The preferred affect is calm, cool and quiet.
- The *abrazo* (see page 71) is not much utilized in Costa Rica.

- It is hotter and more humid in Costa Rica than in many other countries in Latin America. Pay attention to your wardrobe, as frequent changes are needed. Pack accordingly.
- Making a fist with the thumb sticking out between the middle and the index finger is obscene.

## Costa Rican Diplomatic Representation in the United States

Ambassador Tomás Dueñas
2114 S Street NW
Washington, DC 20008
Telephone: (202) 234-2945
embassy@costarica-embassy.org

## Consulates General

Atlanta; Chicago; Houston; Los Angeles; Miami; New Orleans; New York; San Francisco; San Juan, Puerto Rico; and Washington, DC

## U.S. Diplomatic Representation in Costa Rica

Ambassador Peter Cianchette
Calle 120 Avenida O, Pavas
San José, Costa Rica
Telephone: 011-506-519-2000

# ECUADOR

## Basic Information

Population: 14 million
Capital City: Quito
GDP: $7,000

Size: 283,560 sq km, which is slightly smaller than Nevada

Health Risk: high

## Contact Information

Telephone: 011-593 + city code + telephone number

Internet Extension: .ec

## Visa Information

Tourist and business visas may be obtained at the airport upon arrival. Vaccinations against yellow fever are strongly recommended but may or may not actually be required, depending on the previous stops on your journey. Check with the Ecuadoran consulate before leaving.

## Trade

- **Imports:** industrial materials, fuels and lubricants and nondurable consumer goods. About 23 percent of Ecuadoran imports are from the United States.
- **Exports:** petroleum, bananas, cut flowers, shrimp, cacao, coffee, hemp, wood and fish. About 53 percent of exports are to the United States.
- **Exchange Rate:** The U.S. dollar is the only legal currency. There is no local currency.

## About the Country

Ecuador has the most intensely varied landscape in South America. Here you find the Andes, Amazon jungles and beautiful beaches. This country is South America's second-largest producer of oil, which, along with bananas, constitutes the main commerce in the country.

Due to runaway inflation, the U.S. dollar was made

the legal tender in Ecuador in the year 2000. This dollarization has helped to stabilize the economy and encourage growth. The spurt was further encouraged by increasing oil prices. The change over to the dollar has also made Ecuador an attractive location for secreting cash, for drug traffickers wishing to launder currency. The money-laundering law in Ecuador is not effectively enforced.

Political stability is not a notable characteristic of Ecuadorian society. In 2007, a Constituent Assembly was elected to draft Ecuador's twentieth constitution since gaining independence in 1830. Since 1979, three presidents have been thrown out of office. Instability, plus a complex legal system, coupled with corruption leads to a difficult business environment. There was a free trade agreement with the United States, but that was suspended in 2007 because the Ecuadorian government nationalized a U.S. oil company without adequate compensation.

The wealth generated by oil has not trickled down to the masses, and the Ecuadorian people are all aware of this. Change, perhaps violent, is in the offing, so foreign businesses are loath to invest and become enmeshed in the Ecuadoran economy.

## Things to Remember
### LOCAL CUSTOMS
- It is acceptable to discuss business at *comida* if your client brings up the topic. The three-martini lunch or the local equivalent is the rule rather than the exception.
- Anticipate being closely questioned concerning your marital status. North Americans are considered a

great marital catch by Ecuadorian males and females. Such arrangements provide for possible access to a green card and eventually U.S. citizenship.

- Women are rarely seen drinking hard liquor. Wine is acceptable but beer is not.

- A topic for conversation over and beyond the normal range of topics is the Galápagos Islands, which are a part of Ecuador. These are the islands of Darwinian fame. If schedule permits, it is a wonderful side trip by boat directly to the islands, or by air to a neighboring island group where a boat may be secured. Allow about a week.

- The Galápagos are a naturalist's paradise and perhaps the best place in the world to observe wildlife. You can walk up to the enormous seals on the beach or birds in the grass, see unique species, and the wild animals will just sit there for you. Access to these islands is strictly controlled, so reserve early.

**FOOD**

Ecuador is known for its exotic fruits, fish and the countless varieties of Andean potatoes.

Typical menu items in many restaurants include:

- *Cuy:* guinea pig (see page 206 for a full description of this popular dish)
- *Caldo de pata:* a broth containing chunks of boiled cow hooves. Considered a delicacy by Ecuadorians, it is believed to increase virility.
- *Tronquito:* bull penis soup, which is also considered to be a male enhancer

- *Fritada:* roast pork, corn, cheese, avocado, potatoes and plantains all piled on a large plate
- *Locro:* a cheese, avocado and potato soup
- *Yaguarlocro:* a potato soup with chicken intestine and gizzard, and lamb blood on the side

**WARNINGS**

- Crime is a serious problem in Ecuador, and visitors should be alert and cautious. Nonviolent crime is common: hundreds of Americans are robbed every year in Ecuador. Violent crime has increased in recent years. Thieves and small gangs armed with guns or knives are now sometimes active even in smaller cities, such as Otavalo, Manta and Cuenca. Incidents of rape have increased, even in well-traveled tourists areas and when the victims traveled in groups for safety.
- Stay tranquil during meetings. Excessive animation is not customary, and quiet attention and decorum are the norm.
- Relations with neighbor Peru have always been strained, so avoid the topic and remember that the Peru-Ecuador boundary issue is the oldest continuing border dispute in the Western Hemisphere. In 1995 Ecuador finished yet another nasty border war with Peru. The same can be said about the topic of Colombia, with whom the Peruvians are currently conducting border skirmishes. If you have been to Peru or Colombia, or intend to travel to these countries, there is no need to mention that trip to your Ecuadorian clients.

- Ethnicity and class generally are related to shade of skin, with money and power located in white hands and poverty and despair in black.

## Ecuadorian Diplomatic Representation in the United States

Ambassador Luis Benigno Gallegos Chiriboga
2535 15th Street NW
Washington, DC 20009
Telephone: (202) 234-7200
embassy@ecuador.org

## Consulates General

Atlanta; Boston; Chicago; Dallas; Denver; Houston; Jersey City, New Jersey; Los Angeles; Miami; New Orleans; New York; San Francisco; San Juan, Puerto Rico; and Washington, DC

## U.S. Diplomatic Representation in Ecuador

Ambassador Heather Hodges
Avenida 12 de Octubre y Avenida Patria
Quito, Ecuador
Telephone: 011-593-2-256-2890

## Consulates General

Guayaquil

# EL SALVADOR

## Basic Information

Population: 7 million
Capital City: San Salvador

Size: 21,040 sq km, which is slightly smaller than Massachusetts.

GDP: $6,000

Health Risk: high

## Contact Information

Telephone: 011-503 + telephone number

Internet Extension: no specific extension

## Visa Information

A tourist visa may be obtained at the airport upon arrival. Business travelers should consult the El Salvadoran consulate for requirements.

## Trade

- **Imports:** raw materials, consumer goods, capital goods, fuels, foodstuffs, petroleum and electricity. Approximately 30 percent of El Salvadoran imports are from the United States.
- **Exports:** offshore assembly exports with a strong emphasis on textiles, coffee, sugar, shrimp, textiles, chemicals and electricity. Approximately 50 percent of El Salvadoran exports are to the United States.
- **Exchange Rate:** The U.S. dollar is the legal currency of El Salvador.

## About the Country

This is the smallest Mesoamerican country. Nevertheless, it boasts the third-largest economy in the region and it's the only Central American country without a coastline on the Caribbean Sea.

El Salvador, which is Spanish for "the Savior," has

been wrecked by vicious civil war and a succession of natural disasters. This tiny country is the most densely populated nation in Mesoamerica and is highly industrialized. However, social inequality and a susceptibility to earthquakes have shaped much of modern El Salvador. It is known as the "Land of Volcanoes" and is extremely susceptible to hurricanes.

Their recent civil war started in 1979 and lasted officially for twelve years, although it continues today in the form of guerrilla activities. The leadership was not freely elected, but the United States poured $7 billion into El Salvador in an effort to support the government and stop the guerrillas, who the U.S. government characterized as communist. Other sources provided different amounts for this aid, all of which far exceed the $7 billion indicated in official documents. Not only did the rebels survive, however, but the gap between rich and poor widened. Unrest continues, making El Salvador a dangerous place to travel. Foreigners are not targeted, but they can occasionally get caught in the cross fire with unpleasant consequences.

The official language is Spanish, although some of the indigenous population speak Nahua. This language consists of a series of vocalizations that are not related to any European tongue, as Nahua's origins predate Columbus.

English is understood in business centers and by many of the well educated. Although the Salvadorans have traditionally been Roman Catholic, various Protestant groups have gained ground in recent years and now constitute about 10 percent of the population. Some businesspeople are now members of Neopentecostal groups, which equate wealth with God's favor. Do not comment on this if the topic should come up.

## Things to Remember

### LOCAL CUSTOMS

- El Salvador leads the region in cash support from relatives in the United States, with proceeds equivalent to all export income.
- Good eye contact is important in business situations in El Salvador. Maintain a level of contact appropriate to the United States, but don't stare.
- To signal the attention of an El Salvadoran, extend your arm and wriggle your fingers with the palm down. This is not normally performed in a business setting, but rather it is used to summon a waiter or otherwise attract that level of attention.
- Keep your voice down and calm. This is a generally quiet society.
- Handshaking is the usual form of greeting, but unlike in the other countries of Latin America, a lighter or less firm shake is used, which normally lasts longer than a U.S. handshake.

### FOOD

This small country offers little outside of the traditional Latin American repertoire of dishes. Some national specialties include:

- *Pupusa:* a cornmeal tortilla, filled with cheese and beans and shredded pork or chicken
- *Curtido:* the Salvadoran version of sauerkraut and salsa, which is served with *pupusa*
- *Pacalla:* a vegetable fried in egg batter and cornmeal

**WARNINGS**

- The homicide rate in the country increased 25 percent from 2004 to 2007, and El Salvador has one of the highest homicide rates in the world. Violent crimes as well as petty crimes are prevalent throughout El Salvador, and U.S. citizens have been among the victims.

- Do not display anger under any circumstances. Because of the war and the high level of aggressive behavior in its aftermath, many people are armed with pistols, rifles and even machine guns. Many are prepared to shoot with little or no provocation. Stay cool.

- Do not point your fingers at anyone. See above warning.

- Some people merely nod when meeting someone. This is not rudeness but rather a cultural characteristic.

- Men are accustomed to flirting with women. This is the signature national pastime.

- In an exchange between a man and a woman, the woman must extend her hand before the handshake is made. This is considered courteous behavior.

## El Salvadoran Diplomatic Representation
## in the United States

Ambassador René Antonio León Rodríguez

1400 16th Street

Washington, DC 20036

Telephone: (202) 265-9671

http://sansalvador.usembassy.gov

## Consulates General

Boston; Chicago; Dallas; Elizabeth, New Jersey; Houston; Las Vegas; Los Angeles; Miami; New York (2); Nogales, Arizona; Santa Ana, California; San Francisco; Washington, DC; Woodbridge, Virginia; and Woodstock, Georgia

## U.S. Diplomatic Representation in El Salvador

Ambassador (vacant); Chargé d'Affaires Robert Blau

Final Boulevard Santa Elena Sur, Antiguo Cuscatlán, La Libertad

San Salvador, El Salvador

Telephone: 011-503-2278-4444

# GUATEMALA

## Basic Information

Population: 13 million

Capital City: Guatemala City (La Ciudad de Guatemala)

GDP: $5,000

Size: 108,890 sq km, which is just smaller than Tennessee

Health Risk: intermediate

## Contact Information

Telephone: 011-502 + telephone number

Internet Extension: .gt

## Visa Information

Tourist visas have no formal requirements, and the stamp can be obtained at the airport upon arrival. Business travelers require advance planning. Along with your passport, you will need a copy of a letter, in duplicate, from your company indicating its nature and status as well as your planned activities. In addition, you will need a photocopy of your passport, endorsed by the consulate or a notary as being a true representation of the original. The paperwork is best arranged with the Guatemalan consulate weeks before you plan to travel.

## Trade

- **Imports:** fuels, machinery and transport equipment, construction materials, grain, fertilizers and electricity. Approximately 33 percent of Guatemalan imports are from the United States.
- **Exports:** coffee, sugar, petroleum, apparel, bananas, fruits, vegetables and cardamom. Approximately 44 percent of Guatemalan exports are to the United States.
- **Exchange Rate:** 8 Guatemalan quetzals per U.S. dollar

## About the Country

Guatemala is a beautiful country with breathtaking scenery and a strong, vibrant indigenous culture evident. Mountains, lakes and tropical forests are enhanced by wild orchids, and birds are seen everywhere. With a population of 10 million, Guatemala is the most populous country in Central America.

In 2006, the Central America Free Trade Agreement (CAFTA) went into effect between the United States and Guatemala, and it has increased investment in the Guatemalan export economy. However, the distribution of this new income is highly unequal, and about 56 percent of the population lives below the poverty line.

Guatemalans exist in one of the most inequitable societies in the region. Poverty is particularly widespread in the indigenous communities. Infant mortality, malnutrition and illiteracy rates are among the highest in Latin America. Life expectancy is among the lowest. The country is plagued by organized crime families and violent street gangs.

Most of the problems grow out of attempts by the minority Ladinos, who have a mix of European and indigenous heritage, to maintain control of the country without regard to the needs of the indigenous rural population. The Ladinos (the agricultural elite, the military and the government) still control the country in the face of increasing indignation from the indigenous Mayan majority. During the eighties and nineties about a million indigenous Mayans were dispatched to internment camps during the height of the insurgency. The Ladinos believed that the Mayans supported the guerrillas who were trying to take over the government.

Guatemala has had the longest running insurgency in Latin American history, lasting thirty-six years. In 1996, the government signed a peace agreement with the insurgents formally ending the conflict, which had left more than 200,000 people dead or disappeared, creating, by some estimates, 1 million refugees. There is a long tradition of Guatemala being a violence-ridden society.

## Things to Remember
### LOCAL CUSTOMS

- There are a number of growing, very vocal Pentecostal sects in Guatemala, which have influenced the management class and which believe that the wealthy are blessed by God and the poor are not. You will run into this increasingly prominent group, and it will be a topic of conversation among Guatemalan clients. Be prepared for this. The best thing to do is smile, keep quiet and refrain from offering any opinions.

- South Koreans own and manage most of the manufacturing plants in Guatemala. These plants are infamous for their poor working conditions.
- Ladinos tend to offer a firm Latin American handshake, whereas the indigenous Mayans offer a gentler handshake.
- Guatemalans say good-bye by fanning themselves with palm facing the body and fingers held together.

**FOOD**

Guatemalan cuisine is similar to that of other Latin American countries but with Mayan influences. It is based on corn, rice and beans. The coffee is excellent. Among the traditional favorites are the following Mayan variations:

- *Quetzaltenango:* tamales
- *Kak'ik:* a Mayan soup made from turkey and *samat*, which is an herb cultivated for the last ten thousand years. It is also used as a medicine.
- *Jocón:* chicken in green tomato sauce
- *Subanik:* beef, pork and chicken steamed in a spicy sauce

There are two excellent local specialties. The first is the candy manufactured around the town of Antigua. It is appropriately famous. The second is *Quetzalteca*, which is the local moonshine produced from sugarcane. Gallo beer is also popular.

**WARNINGS**

- The number of violent crimes reported by U.S. citizens and other foreigners in Guatemala has remained high in recent years. Incidents include, but are not limited to, assault, theft, armed robbery, carjacking, rape, kidnapping and murder. Guatemala is a deeply troubled society. During the war, Mayans were subject to massacres by the Guatemalan government. The elite Ladinos who conducted this genocide are still in power.

- References to human rights, Mayan culture or racism are inappropriate. You may be shocked by the manner in which you see some Ladinos treating their Mayan serfs, but keep your opinions to yourself.

- Military clothing in any form cannot be brought into the country. You will be arrested if it is found.

## Guatemalan Diplomatic Representation in the United States

Ambassador Francisco Villagrán de León
2220 R Street NW
Washington, DC 20008
Telephone: (202) 745-4952
AmCitsGuatemala@state.gov

## Consulates General

Chicago, Denver, Houston, Los Angeles, Miami, New York, Providence and San Francisco

## U.S. Diplomatic Representation in Guatemala

Ambassador Stephen G. Mcfarland

7-01 Avenida Reforma, Zone 10

Guatemala City, Guatemala

Telephone: 011-502-2326-4000

# HONDURAS

## Basic Information

Population: 8 million. The estimates for this country take into account the effects of excess mortality due to AIDS, which can result in lower life expectancy, higher infant mortality and higher death rates than would normally be anticipated.

Capital City: Tegucigalpa

GDP: $3,000

Size: 112,090 sq km, which is slightly larger than Tennessee

Health Risk: high

## Contact Information

Telephone: 011-504 + telephone number

Internet Extension: .hn

## Visa Information

Neither a tourist nor a business visa is required for citizens of the United States. No vaccinations are required, although a full panel covering the common tropical diseases plus tuberculosis is recommended.

## Trade

- **Imports:** machinery and transport equipment, industrial raw materials, chemical products, fuels and foodstuffs. Approximately 50 percent of Honduran imports are from the United States.

- **Exports:** coffee, shrimp, bananas, gold, palm oil, fruit, lobster and lumber. Approximately 70 percent of Honduran exports are to the United States.
- **Exchange Rate:** 19 Honduran lempiras per U.S. dollar

## About the Country

Honduras is an exciting country in many ways. With beaches, jungles, mountains and a long cultural history, this country has every material attribute a visitor might desire. Physically it is a gem.

The population is youthful, with 50 percent of Hondurans being under the age of nineteen. Approximately 90 percent of the population is mestizo, people with mixed Spanish and indigenous heritage, and 95 percent of Hondurans identify themselves as Catholic. About a quarter of the country's income comes from being a major remittance destination for money sent back to Hondurans by relatives in the United States. These remittance funds, plus coffee and bananas, are the major factors driving the economy.

Tegucigalpa is the capital of Honduras and the name is derived from the ancient Nahunta language.

For all of its beauty, Honduras has its share of problems. It is the second-poorest country in Mesoamerica and one of the poorest countries in the Western Hemisphere, with an extraordinarily unequal distribution of income and massive unemployment. Large international banana and coffee growers control the country. Corruption, a huge wealth gap, crime and natural disasters have rendered Honduras one of the least developed and least secure countries in Mesoamerica.

According to the International Criminal Police Organization (Interpol), the police in Honduras are facing allegations that they are carrying out systematic child executions as part of a prolonged campaign of social cleansing. The bodies of hundreds of murdered children are discovered every year. Interpol also alleges that Honduran girls, thirteen and fourteen years old, are trafficked by organized crime groups from the city of Tegucigalpa, and sold to brothels in Guatemala, El Salvador and Mexico.

## Things to Remember
### LOCAL CUSTOMS

- Single people, particularly foreigners, are viewed with suspicion. You will be asked why you aren't married. The "family man" is perceived to be a stable and trustworthy business partner.
- Unique to Honduras is a gesture used to indicate approval. Put your arm in front of your stomach with your palm facing your body then repeatedly slap your fingers against your palm. It is like a one-handed clap.
- A popular Honduran expression says, "Seek to understand first, then to be understood."

### FOOD

The national dish of Honduras is *plato típico*, or typical plate, which is a plate of beef, fried plantain, beans, pickled cabbage and sour cream. Other typical Honduran dishes are:

- *Baleada:* a flour tortilla filled with beans, cheese and cream

- *Chimole:* the local salsa, possessing varying degrees of heat
- *Pupusa:* cornmeal flat bread stuffed with cheese and refried beans
- *Tiste:* a chocolate drink thickened with corn flour, mixed with milk or water, and similar to the Mexican *atole* (see page 189)
- The local beers include Salva Vida, which means lifesaver, and Barena.

### WARNINGS

- **State Department warning:** "Crime is endemic in Honduras and requires a high degree of caution by U.S. visitors and residents alike. U.S. citizens have been the victims of a wide range of crimes, including murder, kidnapping, rape, assault, and property crimes. Sixty-two U.S. citizens have been murdered in Honduras since 1995; only twenty cases have been resolved. Four U.S citizens were murdered in Honduras in 2007, six in 2006, and ten in 2005. Kidnappings of U.S. citizens have occurred in Honduras, including two incidents in 2007. Poverty, gangs, and low apprehension and conviction rates of criminals contribute to a critical crime rate, including horrific acts of mass murder. With 3,855 murders in 2007, and a population of approximately 7.3 million people, Honduras has one of the world's highest per capita murder rates."
- Criminals and pickpockets target visitors as they enter and depart airports and hotels, so visitors should consider carrying their passports and valuables in a concealed pouch.

• The Pan American Health Organization has identified Honduras as one of ten "priority countries" in an effort to intensify the fight against tuberculosis. Before traveling, make sure you have had your TB series of inoculations, which take some time to become effective. See your internist or an infectious disease specialist as soon as you arrange your trip.

## Honduran Diplomatic Representation in the United States

Ambassador Roberto Flores Bermúdez
Suite 4-M, 3007 Tilden Street NW
Washington, DC 20008
Telephone: (202) 966-7702
www.honduras-embassy.org

## Consulates General

Atlanta, Chicago, Houston, Los Angeles, Miami, New Orleans, New York, Phoenix and San Francisco

## U.S. Diplomatic Representation in Honduras

Ambassador Hugo Llorens
Avenida La Paz, Apartado Postal No. 3453
Tegucigalpa, Honduras
Telephone: 011-504-236-9320

# MEXICO

## Basic Information

Population: 108 million
Capital City: Mexico City (Ciudad de México)

Size: 1,972,550 sq km, which is three times the size of Texas

GDP: $13,000, the highest in Latin America

Health Risk: intermediate

## Contact Information

Telephone: 011-52 + city code + telephone number

Internet extension: .mx

## Visa Information

Business and tourist visas may be obtained upon arrival in Mexico.

## Trade

- **Import:** metalworking machines, steel mill products, agricultural machinery, electrical equipment, car parts for assembly, repair parts for motor vehicles, aircraft, and aircraft parts. Approximately 50 percent of this $283 billion in imports is from the United States.

- **Export:** manufactured goods, oil and oil products, silver, fruits, vegetables, coffee and cotton. Approximately 85 percent of this $271 billion in export trade is conducted with the United States.

- **Exchange Rate:** 11 Mexican pesos per U.S. dollar

## About the Country

Mexico is the United States' major Latin American trading partner for both imports and exports. The total import trade from the sixteen other countries in Latin America does not equal U.S. export trade with Mexico.

The other worthwhile and viable candidates with substantial economies—although not in the same economic class as Mexico—are Brazil, Argentina, Uruguay and Chile. These are our major trading partners in the region. The remaining countries are small and do little significant trade with the United States.

Mexico is discussed as a part of Latin America only in a cultural sense, because geographically, Mexico is part of North America. Based on statistics, this is where you most likely will be doing your business, and on a number of levels it is a great place to both buy and sell. It is also a good place to "cut your teeth" on Latin American business practices, because with the exception of Costa Rica, which has a very small economy, it is the easiest place to do business in Latin America.

After Canada, Mexico is the second-largest export market for the United States. Merchandise being imported into Mexico and exported to the United States is duty-free under NAFTA, giving you an advantage over many of your international competitors. No duty means your landed cost is lower in the United States, and you can maintain lower price points than your competition from other countries. Since it is on our border, market access to Mexico is excellent. The country has a free market economy in the trillion-dollar class, and NAFTA has spurred the growth of a fledgling middle class.

This is the business center of Latin America. The people of Mexico generally welcome the "other North Americans" from the *otro lado* (the other side of the river), if not our politics. There is a Mexican saying: "The only thing that is not negotiable is the virginity of the Virgin of Guadalupe. Everything else is on the table." This attitude makes Mexico the most competitive environment in Latin America. However, the legal system is corrupt and tends to confound North Americans.

The border towns, such as Tijuana, Nuevo Laredo and Nogales, tend not to be considered part of the authentic Mexico and certainly don't reflect the present culture. The same can be said of the Pacific beach resorts, which operate in a dollar economy and have very little to do with modern-day Mexico, Mexican culture or Mexican business practices.

Mexico sits astride the drug highway from South America, which carries product into the United States. Truckloads of illegal money are a corrupting influence in any culture. Thousands of impoverished Guatemalans and other Mesoamericans cross the porous Mexican border looking for work. The country is trying to build fences to keep these undocumented workers out. If these refugees cannot find employment in Mexico, they move on to the United States. Many of the undocumented workers crossing the U.S. border are in fact Mesoamericans and not Mexicans.

There is a major and very much unpublicized population shift going on in Mexico. For hundreds of years Mexicans had large families. An informal survey among sixty-year-olds indicates that seven siblings per family was the norm. In 2008 the birth rate was down to 2.37 children per woman. In five years that number is projected to be 2.2 live births per woman. With childhood deaths and emigration to the *otro lado*, the Mexican population will soon be stable, if not actually shrinking, but the economy is growing at an astonishing pace.

## Things to Remember

### LOCAL CUSTOMS

- All of the cultural details indicated in the first part of the book are valid for Mexico.
- In conversations with Mexicans outside of the capital, you might hear something like "Tomorrow, I am going to Mexico." The flummoxed foreigner should remember that citizens of Mexico refer to their capital simply as Mexico.
- May 5, or *Cinco de Mayo*, is not much celebrated in Mexico, except in the state of Jalisco and in the small ex-pat communities.
- Of interest, Mexico City celebrates Saint Patrick's Day with a parade. This saint is memorialized in honor of the five hundred Irish soldiers that deserted the U.S. Army as a group to fight and die for Mexico during one of the periodic invasions by the United States. There is a memorial to these soldiers in Chapultepec.

### FOOD

Everything you find in the local Mexican restaurants in the United States is available in Mexico, but it's usually more *picante*, or hot. The tortillas are fresh, which makes a big difference. It is believed that Mexicans introduced corn to the Western world, and this is definitely a corn-based cuisine, which ranges from *tamales* to *pozole* to *sopas* (which is not a soup). Some standard authentic Mexican fare includes:

- *Carnitas*: large pieces of pork, deep-fried then sliced and served with tortillas and accompaniment. It is sold by the kilogram in specialty restaurants.

- *Pozole:* a stew of pork and hominy corn flavored with *epazote*, which is an herb.
- *Tacos:* informal food, which we recognize in the United States, is usually eaten standing up or at market stalls that are mostly open only at night. Tacos are not eaten in formal restaurants, except those catering exclusively to tourists. The fillings are prepared while you watch.
- *Atole:* a chocolate-flavored beverage thickened with corn flour
- We are all well aware of tequila, but fewer are acquainted with mescal, produced from the blue agave and considered by Mexicans to be superior in many respects to tequila. Not much mescal is produced and very little is exported. You might consider ordering it and receiving a knowing smile from your clients for your cultural sophistication. Watch for the well-pickled worm floating in the bottle.

The real local moonshine is called *pulque*, made from the fermented juice of the maguey. It is the most traditional native beverage in all of Mesoamerica and consumed fresh in specialty establishments called *pulquerías*. Most of the concoctions are homemade, as they have a poor shelf life and vary in quality.

## WARNINGS

- U.S. citizens residing and traveling in Mexico should exercise caution. In recent years, dozens of U.S. citizens have been kidnapped there, and many cases remain unresolved. Refrain from displaying expensive-looking jewelry, large amounts of money or other valuable items.

- According to *The CIA World Factbook*: "Major drug syndicates control the majority of drug trafficking throughout the country; producer and distributor of ecstasy; significant money-laundering center; major supplier of heroin and largest foreign supplier of marijuana and methamphetamine to the U.S. market." Much of the violence is along the border shared with the United States.
- Mexicans are North Americans and not South or Mesoamericans. Be sensitive to this in your conversations. A mistake in this area is a clear sign of cultural insensitivity.

## Mexican Diplomatic Representation in the United States

Ambassador Arturo Sarukhan Casamitjana
1911 Pennsylvania Avenue NW
Washington, DC 20006
Telephone: (202) 728-1600
www.embassyofmexico.org

## Consulates General (offering a full range of consular services)

Atlanta; Austin; Boston; Chicago; Dallas; Denver; El Paso, Houston, and Laredo, Texas; Los Angeles; Miami; New Orleans; New York; Nogales, Arizona; Omaha; Orlando; Phoenix; Sacramento; San Antonio; San Diego; San Francisco; San Jose; San Juan, Puerto Rico

## Consulates (offering a limited range of consular services)

Albuquerque; Brownsville, Del Rio, Eagle Pass, Laredo, McAllen, and Presidio, Texas; Calexico, Fresno, Oxnard,

San Bernardino, and Santa Ana, California; Detroit;
Douglas, Tucson, and Yuma, Arizona; Indianapolis;
Kansas City, Missouri; Las Vegas; Little Rock, Arkansas;
New Orleans; Omaha; Orlando; Philadelphia; Portland,
Oregon; Raleigh; Saint Paul, Minnesota; Salt Lake City;
Seattle

## U.S. Diplomatic Representation in Mexico

Ambassador Antonio O. Garza Jr.
Paseo de la Reforma 305, Colonia Cuauhtemoc
México, Distrito Federal 06500
Telephone: 011-52-55-5080-2000

## Consulates General

Ciudad Juárez, Guadalajara, Monterrey, Tijuana, Her-
mosillo, Matamoros, Mérida, Nogales and Nuevo Laredo

# NICARAGUA

## Basic Information

Population: 6 million
Capital City: Managua
GDP: $3,000
Size: 129,494 sq km, which is just smaller than New
York State
Health Risk: intermediate

## Contact Information

Telephone: 011 + 505 + telephone number
Internet Extension: .ni

## Visa Information

For about $10 on arrival, U.S. citizens with a passport can obtain a tourist card, which is good for stays of one month. Business travelers will require a letter from their employer or from a company in Nicaragua. There is a $35 tax for all visitors when they leave the country.

## Trade

- **Imports:** consumer goods, machinery and equipment, raw materials and petroleum products. Approximately 20 percent of Nicaragua's imports come from the United States.
- **Exports:** coffee, beef, shrimp, lobster, tobacco, sugar, gold and peanuts. Approximately 60 percent of Nicaragua's goods are exported to the United States.
- **Exchange Rate:** 19 Nicaraguan gold córdobas per U.S. dollar

## About the Country

Nicaraguans are genuinely friendly people, but a bit more reserved than most Latin Americans. The people are hard workers who trudge on in spite of the oppressive heat and humidity. Along the coast, the temperature *averages* 89°F.

Nicaragua is a very young society, with 60 percent of the population being under the age of seventeen. It is the largest country in Mesoamerica and contains the largest freshwater body in Central America, Lago de Nicaragua. There is equal opportunity in Nicaragua in education and employment, at least under the law.

The U.S.–Central America Free Trade Agreement (CAFTA) has been in effect since April 2006 and has expanded export opportunities for many agricultural and manufactured goods. Energy shortages fueled by increasingly high oil prices remain an impediment to growth.

The country also endures widespread underemployment, with one of the highest degrees of income inequality in the world and the third-lowest per capita income in the Western Hemisphere. There is wealth, but it is closely held in the hands of the rich farm families. Fifty percent of the population is unemployed or underemployed. In an endemically corrupt region and perhaps the most corrupt country in Latin America, Nicaragua is the land of the now famous Sandinistas and various other guerrilla groups.

Street names and address numbers don't exist in Managua, the country's capital, which makes getting around a bit of a challenge. Taking a taxi is the only practical way to travel, unless your client has offered to pick you up.

## Things to Remember
### LOCAL CUSTOMS

- Casual physical contact is taken for granted here, and many of the people are famously affable and love to talk. If you are a woman and a male is overly physical with you, back off quickly or your response can become misinterpreted.
- Punctuality is not a concern here. An hour's delay should not be taken as a significant event. Bring reading material and be patient.
- Baseball makes for a good safe topic for discussion. A number of Nicaraguans play in the professional

leagues, and it has become a very popular sport in this country.

- Because of their affability, Nicaraguans have trouble saying no to things. Even if pressed for a decision, they may simply change the topic. If you see this happening, understand what they are really saying. If you are persistent over time and still cannot elicit a response one way or the other, it is safe to assume that they are not interested in doing business with you.

## FOOD

There are few food items that are peculiar to Nicaragua. The high poverty level makes eating in restaurants a rarity for most of the locals, but the food stalls along the streets are popular. If you see a stand with a crowd in front, it is usually safe. Avoid the fruit drinks because of the dangers inherent in the water or ice that's used in their preparation.

*Gallo pinto* is the national dish of Nicaragua, and it is a plate of rice and beans along with salad, fried banana and fried cheese. Skip the salad because of the highly questionable water used to clean the greens. Stay with bottled beverages with no ice.

## WARNINGS

- Violent crime in Managua and other cities is increasing, and street crimes are common. Pickpocketing and occasional armed robberies occur on crowded buses and particularly in the large Mercado Oriental.

- The carnage in the streets during the recent civil war, 1978–2000, was horrible and is not a subject for discussion.
- Be careful that what you are proposing is not, even in a limited or temporary sense, a labor-saving process. High unemployment rates have made local managers feel quite insecure. Products that save time and money are not viable. Products that produce jobs gain wide acceptance.
- Prolonged eye contact should be studiously avoided in this culture.
- In spite of the legal equality between the sexes, Nicaragua is perhaps the most chauvinistic country in Latin America, so avoid the topic of women and equality between the sexes.
- Holidays usually involve an absence of more than the official day. Sometimes as much as a week is taken off around the legal holidays.

## Nicaraguan Diplomatic Representation in the United States

Ambassador Arturo Cruz Sequeira Jr.
1627 New Hampshire Avenue NW
Washington, DC 20009
Telephone: (202) 939-6570
http://nicaraguaembassy.com

## Consulates General

Houston, Los Angeles, Miami, New York and San Francisco

## U.S. Diplomatic Representation in Nicaragua

Ambassador Robert J. Callahan
Kilometer 4.5 Carretera Sur

Managua, Nicaragua
Telephone: 011-505-266-3861

# PANAMA

## Basic Information

Population: 3 million
Capital City: Panama City
Size: 78,200 sq km, which is slightly smaller than South Carolina
GDP: $9,000
Health Risk: intermediate

## Contact Information

Telephone: 011-507 + telephone number
Internet Extension: .pa

## Visa Information

Tourist cards may be obtained at the airport upon arrival. Business travelers should contact the Panamanian consulate for visa requirements.

## Trade

- **Import:** capital goods, foodstuffs, consumer goods and chemicals. Approximately 27 percent of Panamanian imports come from the United States.
- **Export:** bananas, shrimp, sugar, coffee and clothing. Approximately 40 percent of Panamanian exports are to the United States.
- **Exchange Rate:** 1 Panamanian balboa per U.S. dollar. The Panamanian currency is kept at parity with the dollar.

## About the Country

Panama straddles the crossroads of both the North and South American continents and the Atlantic and Pacific oceans. It is one of the smallest countries in Meso-america, but it is home to the Panama Canal, which has brought substantial business to this tiny country. Most businesspeople speak English, and the country demonstrates less of the typical Latin America cultural characteristics than most other Latin American nations.

This country has the largest rain forest in the Western Hemisphere outside the Amazon Basin, and its jungle is home to an abundance of tropical plants, animals and birds—some of them to be found nowhere else in the world. In spite of these attractions, which seem to be a well-kept secret, the country is not a popular tourist destination for North Americans.

The dollarized economy rests primarily on a service sector that accounts for three-quarters of the national income. Services include operating the Panama Canal, banking, and the Colón Free Trade Zone. The zone, at the hub of this commerce, is also a center for narcotics, money laundering and other nefarious endeavors.

Boxing is the significant national sport, and the country has produced a substantial number of world champions.

## Things to Remember
### LOCAL CUSTOMS

- Always include your client's spouse in invitations to business dinners. This is a peculiar custom in Panama and not much utilized in the remainder of Latin America.

- Good conversation topics include family, hobbies, basketball, baseball and boxing. Soccer is not the only subject for male bonding, as it is in many other Latin American countries.

**FOOD**

The food is similar to that of other Latin American countries, but it is not particularly spicy. Among the local specialties you might encounter are:

- *Carimanola:* a fried roll made from ground and boiled yucca, filled with chopped meat and boiled eggs.
- *Patacones:* green fried plantains cut crossways in pieces, salted, pressed and fried
- *Tajadas:* ripe plantains cut in slices and baked with cinnamon
- *Sao:* raw pork feet, pickled using vinegar and onion slivers. This delicacy should be avoided at all cost, as the current trichinosis situation has not been evaluated.

**WARNINGS**

- The city of Colón is a high-crime area.
- Bad conversation topics are race problems and Manuel Noriega. Noriega was the previous chief executive officer in Panama and was connected to the drug trade and other criminal activities. He was removed from power in 1989 through U.S. military intervention.

• Dengue fever is endemic, as is yellow fever. Appropriate inoculations are strongly recommended.

## Panamanian Diplomatic Representation in the United States

Ambassador Federico Humbert Arias
2862 McGill Terrace NW
Washington, DC 20008
Telephone: (202) 483-1407
www.embassyofpanama.org

## Consulates General

Atlanta; Honolulu; Houston; Miami; New Orleans; New York; Philadelphia; San Diego; San Francisco; San Juan, Puerto Rico; and Tampa

## U.S. Diplomatic Representation in Panama

Ambassador Barbara J. Stephenson
Edificio 783, Avenida Demetrio Basilio Lakas
Panama City, Panama
Telephone: 011-507-207-7000

# PARAGUAY

## Basic Information

Population: 7 million
Capital City: Asunción
GDP: $4,000
Size: 78,200 sq km, which is slightly smaller than California
Health Risk: intermediate

## Contact Information

Telephone: 011-595 + telephone number

Internet Extension: .py

## Visa Information

Prior to departure, U.S. citizens traveling to Paraguay must submit completed visa applications in person or by secure messenger to the Paraguayan embassy or one of the consulates and pay a fee. Travelers entering and departing Paraguay with U.S. passports will be fingerprinted.

## Trade

- **Imports:** road vehicles, consumer goods, tobacco, petroleum products and electrical imports come from the United States. Exports to Paraguay from the United States are less than 1 percent.
- **Exports:** Soybeans, feed, cotton, meat, edible oils, electricity, wood and leather. Exports from Paraguay to the United States are less than 1 percent.

  **Note:** The country does virtually no business with the United States on the exporting side and extremely little on the importing side.
- **Exchange Rate:** 5,000 Paraguayan guaraní per U.S. dollar

## About the Country

Paraguay is a small, landlocked country located in the heart of South America, between Brazil, Argentina and Bolivia. This beautiful green land has a wealth of natural, cultural and historical heritage. The population of 7 million lives in an area about the size of California. Paraguay is one of South America's least densely populated countries.

The country owes its diverse culture to the mixture of traditional Spanish descendents with the native Guaraní. Up to 95 percent of Paraguayans are mestizo, people of mixed Spanish and indigenous descent, and 90 percent are Catholic. Many speak the language of the indigenous Guaraní. The rest are bilingual or only speak Spanish. As in Brazil, there is a Japanese community, which is a legacy of post–World War II migration.

Paraguay has a market economy distinguished by a large "informal sector," which means that it is essentially a black market economy with little if any reporting of business transactions to the government. This segment of the economy encompasses both the export of imported consumer goods to neighboring countries, as well as the activities of small business and urban street vendors. Paraguay is reputed to be the smuggling capital of South America, which seems counterintuitive considering that, along with Bolivia, it is one of the two landlocked countries on the continent.

### Things to Remember
#### LOCAL CUSTOMS
- You will be asked personal questions by friendly people. The more detailed your response, the better you will get along in business. They want to know all about you.
- Soccer is a major topic of conversation.
- Use more eye contact than in other Latin American countries. Not maintaining eye contact makes you appear shifty and untrustworthy in this culture.

- The traditional Paraguayan formal shirt, or *ao poí*, can be worn to the office or formal social occasions such as weddings.
- When there is heavy rain, it isn't uncommon for the locals to stay at home in spite of any previous commitments.
- Deadlines are not taken seriously, and everything is usually left till the last minute, or *a última hora*.
- Women's equality is not taken as seriously in Paraguay as it is in the United States.
- Indigenous Guaraní, whose culture is little valued in spite of numerous efforts to revive it, are often looked down upon by the Ladino population.

## FOOD

The customary Latin American dishes, with a strong emphasis on corn and cornmeal, are encountered on the street or in restaurants. In addition, you might find the following Paraguayan specialties:

- *Chipas:* cornbread mixed with egg and cheese
- *Sopa paraguaya:* a soup of mashed corn, cheese, milk and onions.
- *Soo-yosopy:* a soup of cornmeal and ground beef
- *Surubí:* a type of catfish taken from local waters
- *Yerba maté:* tea brewed from dried leaves from the yerba maté tree
- The local moonshine is called *caña*, which is clear alcohol distilled from sugarcane and honey

## WARNINGS

- The World Health Organization in 2008 issued *a health alert for Paraguay*, in an attempt to stop a new outbreak of dengue fever. Travelers should take care to protect themselves against mosquito bites while in the country and consult a doctor immediately if they develop any flulike symptoms. It is a serious matter.

- Perhaps even more worrisome, the deadliest yellow fever outbreak in sixty years is ongoing. Travelers to Paraguay are strongly advised to obtain a vaccination at least two weeks before arriving in the country.

- Crime has increased in recent years, with criminals often targeting those thought to be wealthy.

- According to the CIA, the unruly region at the convergence of the Argentina-Brazil-Paraguay borders is the center of money laundering, smuggling, arms and illegal narcotics trafficking and fund-raising for extremist organizations. This is literally a lawless region.

- You may pick up an unwelcome visitor in the form of a tiny foot flea known locally as *pique*, which will usually collect around your toes. They will lay eggs in your feet if not immediately and forcibly removed. The best way to get rid of them is for you or a friend to pierce the afflicted site with a needle and pour hydrogen peroxide over the area. Then dig the dead bugs out. Do this before you leave the country, because you don't want the fleas to invade your home when you return.

## Paraguayan Diplomatic Representation in the United States

Ambassador James Spalding Hellmers
2400 Massachusetts Avenue NW
Washington, DC 20008

Telephone: (202) 483-6960
secretaria@embaparusa.gov.py

**Consulates General**
Los Angeles, Miami and New York

**U.S. Diplomatic Representation in Paraguay**
Ambassador Liliana Ayalde
1776 Avenida Mariscal López, Casilla Postal 402
Asunción, Paraguay
Telephone: 011-595 (21) 213-715

# PERU

**Basic Information**
Population: 29 million
Capital City: Lima
GDP: $8,000
Size: 1,285,220 sq km, which is just smaller than
    Alaska
Health Risk: very high

**Contact Information**
Telephone: 011-51 + city code + telephone number
Internet Extension: .pe

**Visa Information**
A tourist card may be secured at the airport upon deplaning. Business visas require a copy of the contract for services rendered between the foreign company and the legal Peruvian entity receiving the services. It must be a legally notarized copy or authorized by a public official of

the General Director of Migration and Naturalization. In addition, you will need a document of designation issued by your company, duly legalized in the Peruvian consulate and endorsed by External Relations, with instructions for type of services to be rendered within the country. If in English, these documents must be accompanied by an official notarized translation into Spanish.

## Trade

- **Imports:** petroleum products, plastics, machinery, vehicles, iron and steel, wheat and paper. Approximately 16 percent of imports are from the United States.
- **Exports:** copper, gold, zinc, crude petroleum, coffee, potatoes, asparagus, textiles and guinea pigs. Approximately 24 percent of exports are sent to the United States.
- **Exchange Rate:** 3 Peruvian nuevo sol per U.S. dollar

## About the Country

Peru is well known for its ruins at the lost city of Machu Picchu, an incredible sight located at an elevation where altitude sickness can be a problem. However, Lima, Peru's capital, is at sea level and more than half of the country is covered by jungle and rain forest.

Growth prospects for the country depend on the export of minerals, textiles and agricultural products. The country is rich in copper, silver, lead, zinc, oil and gold and has rich fishing grounds, yet it is rife with social and economic inequality. The small elite of Spanish heritage control the wealth and power, while the indigenous Peruvians live in desperate poverty.

The country is second behind Colombia in the production of the world's cocaine crop, which finances the local Shining Path and Tupac Amaru Revolutionary Movement guerrillas. The resulting social and safety problems are evident. Because the economy and infrastructure have been neglected, foreign companies have customarily avoided involvement in Peru. The political situation remains unstable.

## Things to Remember
### LOCAL CUSTOMS

- Business clubs utilized primarily for business lunches are very conservative venues. The dress codes, in spite of the heat, do not allow men to remove jackets when dining. Decorum rules.

- Corruption exists to a limited extent but is not as endemic and pervasive as it is in other Latin American countries. Twenty dollars is an average *mordida* (see page 58). The typical "bites" range from $10 to get customs agents to clear your merchandise or for a manager to speed up installation of telephone service, to $20 to obtain a building permit. Other activities require higher but not exorbitant payments.

### FOOD

- *Cuy:* cooked guinea pig, either fried or baked, and served whole (head, fur, paws, and all) on a platter with potatoes and vegetables. You are unlikely to find it served at a business lunch or dinner, but it may well appear when you are taken out by your clients to participate in the local cuisine. This may sometimes be done as a sort of joke to shock the visitor. Try to take a few bites if only to provide a credible hardship story for your peers when you get home.

- *Ceviche:* the national dish of Peru, composed of raw seafood marinated in lemon, very hot peppers, coriander, and garlic, which chemically cook the fish.
- There are more than two thousand varieties of botanically distinct indigenous potatoes in Peru. Typically, potatoes and rice are presented at every repast. In fact, up to five different types of potatoes may be provided at a single meal. Each type of potato served will be unique in color, flavor and texture, and eating them is an educational experience. You will never again look at the potato as a pedestrian vegetable.

## WARNINGS

- **State Department warning:** "Violent crime, including carjacking, assault, and armed robbery, is common in Lima and other large cities. Resistance to violent crime often provokes greater violence, while victims who do not resist usually do not suffer serious physical harm. 'Express kidnappings,' in which criminals kidnap victims and seek to obtain funds from their bank accounts via automatic teller machines, occur frequently. Thieves often smash car windows at traffic lights to grab jewelry, purses, backpacks, or other visible items from a car. This type of assault is very common on main roads leading to Lima's Jorge Chavez International Airport, specifically along De la Marina and Faucett Avenues and Via de Evitamiento, but it can occur anywhere in congested traffic, particularly in downtown Lima." This is an excerpt from the much longer warning on Peru that can be found at http://travel .state.gov/travel/cis_pa_tw.

- Unlike in Mexico and some of the other more exuberant Latin American nations, displays of affection between colleagues are subdued.

- Do not look directly in the eyes of someone of the opposite sex, since it may be misinterpreted.

- Peruvians will go to great lengths to avoid a direct no. Your option is to be patient and keep trying. A conversation option is to say after repeated delays, "Would it be better for me to get back to you next year?" That will give them the opportunity to say yes.

- Approximately 15 percent of the roads in Peru are paved. The remainder are dirt tracks. Peru's climate can be divided into two seasons—wet and dry. The dry season falls between the summer months of December and April. During the rest of the year, the coastal fog arrives and the sun is rarely seen. Transportation is nearly impossible in this wet season, when it can rain sixteen days a month. Avoid May through November for business purposes.

- The three most vexing problems with doing business in Peru are policies that seem to change on a day-to-day basis, a more than normally inefficient government bureaucracy and byzantine, even by Latin American standards, tax regulations. These taxing policies are extremely complex and in some cases change on a month-to-month basis. Consult a local tax attorney for information on your situation.

**Peruvian Diplomatic Representation
in the United States**

Ambassador Luis Valdivieso Montano
1700 Massachusetts Avenue NW
Washington, DC 20036
Telephone: (202) 833-9860
mtalavera@embassyofperu.us

**Consulates General**

Atlanta; Boston; Chicago; Denver; Hartford; Houston;
Los Angeles; Miami; New York; Paterson, New Jersey; San
Francisco and Washington, DC

**U.S. Diplomatic Representation in Peru**

Ambassador P. Michael McKinley
Avenida La Encalada, Cuadra 17s/n, Surco
Lima 33 Peru
Telephone: 011-51-1-434-3000

# URUGUAY

**Basic Information**

Population: 3 million
Capital City: Montevideo
GDP: $13,000
Size: 176,220 sq km, which is just smaller than the
state of Washington
Health Risk: normal

**Contact Information**

Telephone: 011 + 598 + city code + telephone number
Internet Extension: .uy

**Visa Information**

An entry card may be obtained at the airport upon arrival for tourist and business travelers.

**Trade**

- **Imports:** crude petroleum and petroleum products, machinery, chemicals, road vehicles, paper and plastics. Uruguay imports about 8 percent from the United States.
- **Exports:** meat, rice, leather products, wool, fish and dairy products. Uruguay exports about 12 percent to the United States.
- **Exchange Rate:** 24 Uruguayan pesos per U.S. dollar

**About the Country**

One of the smallest countries in South America, Uruguay is one of the very few countries in the world where there is no personal income tax, but rather a tax is imposed on individual net worth. This practice encourages neither savings nor accumulation of wealth. If you have money, the government seems to be saying, spend it or be taxed on it. The economy is driven by the agricultural sector, and the workforce is well educated and up to U.S. or European standards. Half of the population lives in Montevideo, the capital. This country has the highest percentage in Latin America of people claiming European descent.

The people take a pragmatic and utilitarian approach to life. Uruguay is the second least corrupt state in Latin America after Chile, with a secular democratic government. The country's political and labor conditions are among the freest on the continent. Culturally, Uruguay is one of the least Latin American countries in South

America and one of the closest to the North American business model.

Uruguay has traditionally been wealthier than many other countries in South America and is known for its advanced education, social security system (a unique concept in Latin America) and rational law enforcement. This country set up the first social net in Latin America to protect its citizens, funded by taxes on corporations. There is a middle class, and the country is largely free of serious income inequality and therefore free from any serious social problems. It is one of the very few Latin American countries not to have a health hazard designation by the U.S. government. Law-and-order issues are under control.

U.S. trade thrives, a result of high commodity prices for Uruguayan exports, a strong peso, duty-free trade arrangements and growth in the region. More than one hundred U.S companies have operations in Uruguay, although most of the country is grassland used for cattle and sheep.

The challenges Uruguay faces in promoting its local market are both its small size and the lack of trade-related financing. Uruguay is still largely unknown to U.S. companies. The country is a land of immigrants: Spanish, French, British and Italians have replaced the indigenous people through natural attrition. Recently, groups from Russia and the Middle East have mixed into this highly desirable melting pot.

## Things to Remember
### LOCAL CUSTOMS
- The "ch-ch" sound is used to get someone's attention or to get a bus to stop.

- American jeans are very popular here and they make a wonderful gift for subsequent visits. The standard type of gifts discussed in Chapter 7 will be sufficient for the initial visit.

## FOOD

The ubiquitous Uruguayan dish is the *Asado*, consisting of three meats cooked over a wood fire in an oven called a *parrillero*. Eating this dish is as much a social gathering as a dinner. There is much talk and bonhomie. Some other popular dishes include:

- *Dulce de leche:* sweet heavy cream, which shows up in many desserts, usually with fruit
- *Maté:* herbal tea normally served with a meal
- *Chivito:* meat sandwich containing a number of additions and that tastes like our club sandwich
- *Clericó:* wine and fruit juice combination similar to sangria

## WARNINGS

- This is a small country with very little capital. Financing, sometimes creative, will be the key to your success in this business environment.
- In Uruguay, perhaps more than in other Latin American countries, a highly educated businessperson may be working at a low-level position due to factors unrelated to competency. Do not ask questions about this.
- A Uruguayan may invite you to his home for coffee after dinner. This runs contrary to the custom

in other Latin American countries. As a matter of courtesy, don't stay late on a work night.

## Uruguayan Diplomatic Representation in the United States

Ambassador Carlos Alberto Gianelli Drois
1913 I Street NW
Washington, DC 20006
Telephone: (202) 331-1313

## Consulates General

Chicago; Los Angeles; Miami; New York; San Juan, Puerto Rico; and Washington, DC
uruwashi@uruwashi.org

## U.S. Diplomatic Representation in Uruguay

Ambassador (vacant); Chargé d'Affaires Robin H. Matthewman
Lauro Muller 1776
Montevideo, Uruguay 11200
Telephone: 011-598-2-418-7777

# VENEZUELA

## Basic Information

Population: 26 million
Capital City: Caracas
GDP: $13,000
Size: 912,050 sq km, which is twice the size of California
Health Risk: high

## Contact Information

Telephone: 011 + city code + telephone number

Internet Extension: .ve

## Visa Information

A tourist card can be obtained at the airport upon arrival. Business travelers should contact the nearest Venezuelan consulate to obtain the latest list of visa requirements.

## Trade

- **Imports:** raw materials, machinery and equipment, transport equipment and construction materials. Approximately 30 percent is imported from the United States.
- **Exports:** petroleum, aluminum, steel, chemicals, agricultural products and basic manufactures. Approximately 48 percent is exported to the United States.
- **Exchange Rate:** 22 Venezuelan bolívares fuertes per U.S. dollar. This is a new currency as of January 1, 2008.

## About the Country

Venezuela is a beautiful country. The topography runs from snow in the Andes to tropical jungles in the south. The beaches are comparable to the best in the Caribbean. There are two seasons. The dry season extends from December to April, the wet one from May to November.

Angel Falls is located on the Amazon River and constitutes the border with Brazil. It is by a large margin the world's highest and least accessible waterfall. The falls are best reached from Manaus, Brazil, by riverboat up the Amazon, which is a trip of about a week's duration.

Venezuela has some of the world's largest proven oil deposits as well as huge quantities of coal, iron ore, bauxite and gold. Oil drives the economy and accounts for about two-thirds of exports. Gasoline in Venezuela is very inexpensive. Yet most Venezuelans live in poverty.

With Hugo Chávez as its president and a socialist revolution, Venezuela is enjoying a windfall from high oil prices. According to the CIA, Sr. Chávez has introduced twenty-first-century socialism, "which purports to alleviate social ills while at the same time attacking globalization and undermining regional stability. Current concerns include a weakening of democratic institutions, political polarization, a politicized military, drug-related violence along the Colombian border, increasing internal drug consumption . . . Emboldened by his December 2006 reelection, President Hugo Chávez nationalized firms in the petroleum, communications, and electricity sectors, which reduced foreign influence in the economy."

## Things to Remember
### LOCAL CUSTOMS

- There is a dichotomy in the business culture. The older, forty-plus businesspeople behave like typical Latin American executives with their emphasis on friendship and lack of concern with meeting commitments. The younger executives behave like typical North American MBAs.
- It is normal to invite your client to lunch after your morning meeting. If the invitation is accepted, it's a portent of good things to come. Unlike in other Latin American nations, it is customary in Venezuela

to discuss business during lunch, as an extension of the meeting, while dinner conversation is reserved for relationship building.

- Speeding motorcycles with multiple passengers are endemic.

## FOOD

There are a number of Venezuelan specialties. In addition to the standard Latin American fare, you'll find:

- *Perros calientes:* also known as hot dogs
- *Pabellón:* shredded meat plated with rice, black beans, and banana
- *Hallaca:* traditional Christmas dish composed of various meats stuffed into corn dough, which is then packaged in a banana leaf and boiled
- *Cachapa:* sweet corn pancake served with cheese
- *Arepas:* circular cornmeal biscuit

## WARNINGS

- **State Department warning:** "Venezuela and its capital, Caracas, have one of the highest per capita murder rates in the world. Virtually all murders go unsolved. The poor neighborhoods that cover the hills around Caracas are extremely dangerous." Please consult the State Department at http://travel.state.gov/travel for additional information on this topic.
- Venezuelans take politics seriously. The society is polarized between "Chavists," who support President Chávez, and "Antichavists," who oppose him, and you might never know the real orientation of your client. Avoid taking a position.

- According to the CIA: "Venezuela is a source, transit, and destination country for women and children trafficked for the purposes of sexual exploitation and forced labor . . . [and] does not fully comply with the minimum standards for the elimination of trafficking and is not making significant efforts to do so." Young teen females literally can be purchased for about $150 from white slavers throughout Caracas.

## Venezuelan Diplomatic Representation in the United States

Ambassador (vacant); Chargé d'Affaires Angelo Rivero Santos
1099 30th Street NW
Washington, DC 20007
Telephone: (202) 342-2214

## Consulates General

Boston; Chicago; Houston; Miami; New Orleans; New York; San Francisco; and San Juan, Puerto Rico
www.embavenez-us.org

## U.S. Diplomatic Representation in Venezuela

Ambassador (vacant); Chargé d'Affaires John Caulfield
Calle F con Calle Suapure
Urbanización Colinas de Valle Arriba
Caracas 1080, Venezuela
Telephone: 011-58-212-975-9234

# APPENDIX A

# Selected Business-Related Terms in Spanish

What follows is a list of common Spanish terms utilized in the business environment. Spanish terminology that has a very close English equivalent has not been included, as it should be understood without assistance.

| | |
|---|---|
| Abstract | Resumen |
| Accounting | Contabilidad |
| Advertising | Publicidad |
| Agency | Representación |
| Arbitration | Arbitraje |
| Assets | Activos |
| Audit | Auditoría |
| Authority | Autoridad |
| Average (mathematical) | Promedio |
| Balance Sheet | Balanza general |
| Bankruptcy | Quiebra; Insolvencia |
| Benefits | Beneficios |
| Board of Directors | Mesa directiva |

Boilerplate .............................. Lenguaje estandarizado
en documentos legales

Bonus ..................................... Gratificación;
Bonificación

Bookkeeping ......................... Teneduría de libros;
Contabilización

Brand...................................... Marca de venta;
Marca de fábrica

Breach of Contract ............... Incumplimiento
de contrato

Broker.................................... Corredor or bolsista;
Agiotista

Budget ................................... Presupuesto

Business................................. Negocio

Business agent ...................... Agent comercial

Business law ......................... Derecho mercantil

Business plan........................ Plan de negocio

Cash basis............................. Base de efectivo

Certified public .................... Contadores públicos
accountants                         autorizados

Checks................................... Cheques

Chief executive officer .......... Funcionaro ejecutivo
principal

Chief information officer...... Funcionario de
comunicación principal

Claim..................................... Reclamación

| | |
|---|---|
| Claims | Demandas |
| Collateral | Colateral |
| Commercial paper | Papel comercial |
| Common law | Ley común |
| Competitive advantage | Ventaja competitiva |
| Contract | Contrato |
| Credit Cards | Tarjetas de crédito |
| Currency | Moneda |
| Current assets | Activo circulante |
| Current liabilities | Pasivo circulante |
| Customer service | Servicio al cliente |
| Customs duties | Derechos de aduana |
| Damages | Daños |
| Deed | Escritura or contrato |
| Direct mail | Correo directo |
| Discount pricing | Precios de descuento |
| Discount stores | Tiendas de descuento |
| E-Commerce | Comercio electrónico |
| Economies of scale | Economías de escala |
| Electronic Commerce | Comercialización electrónica |
| Email | Correo electrónico |
| Employee benefits | Beneficios a empleados |
| Employment at will | Empleado de plazo indeterminado |

Employment interview ......... Entrevista de empleo

Entrepreneurs........................ Empresarios

Exchange rate........................ Tipo de cambio

Expenses............................... Gastos

Exporting ............................. Exportación

Feedback............................... Reacción

First-line managers................ Administradores de
primera línea

Flowchart ............................. Organigrama

Foreign exchange.................. Intercambio de divisas

Franchise.............................. Franquicia

Free trade............................. Libre comercio

General expenses .................. Gastos generales

General partnership.............. Sociedad colectiva;
Agrupación

Generic products................... Productos genéricos

Goal...................................... Meta;
Objectivo

Gross profit........................... Ganancia bruta

Hidden agenda ...................... Agenda oculta

Human resources .................. Recursos humanos

Inflation ............................... Inflación

Injunction ............................ Mandamiento judicial

Insurance ............................. Seguro

Intellectual property............. Propiedad intelectual

Internal auditors ................... Auditores internos

International Law ................. Ley internacional

Interpersonal skills .............. Habilidades interpersonales

Job description ...................... Descripción de trabajo

Joint venture ......................... Empresa conjunta

Just-in-time system .............. Tiempo de reorden

Knowledge............................. Conocimiento

Lead time .............................. Plazo de entrega

Lease..................................... Arrendamiento

Liabilities.............................. Pasivos

Licensing............................... Otorgamiento de licencias

Limited liability .................... Compañía de
company (LLC)                     responsabilidad limitada

Limited partnership.............. Sociedad en comandita

Line of credit........................ Línea de crédito

Liquidity............................... Liquidez

Mail-order store.................... Empresa de ventas por correo

Management .......................... Administración

Management .......................... Sistema de administración
information system              de información

Market globalization............. Globalización de mercado

Market share.......................... Porcentaje de mercado

Marketing.............................. Mercadotecnia

Marketing research ............... Investigación de mercadeo

Mass production .................... Producción en gran
escala

Materials handling ............... Manejo de materiales

Media ................................... Medios publicitarios
de comunicación

Mediation ............................. Mediación;
Arbitraje;
Intervención

Merchant wholesalers ........... Comerciante de mayoreo

Merger .................................. Fusión;
Consolidación

Middle managers .................. Administradores
intermedios

Mission statement ................ Declaración de objetivos

National brand ...................... Marca nacional

Net income ........................... Ingreso neto

News release ......................... Difusión de noticias

Operating expenses .............. Gastos operativos

Operating systems ................ Sistemas operativos

Operational plans ................. Plan operacional

Outsourcing .......................... Contratación de
terceros para servicios o
manufactura

Owners' equity ...................... Participación del dueño

Parent company .................... Compañía controladora

Partnership ........................... Sociedad;
Asociación

Pay for performance.............. Pago por rendimiento

Performance appraisal .......... Evaluación de rendimiento

Personal property.................. Propiedad personal;
Bienes inmuebles
e intangibles

Philanthropic ........................ Filantrópico

Pie chart ............................... Diagrama de sectores

Pollution............................... Contaminación

Position paper ...................... Documento de postura;
Actitud

Power of attorney.................. Carta poder

Premiums............................. Primas;
Premios

Profit..................................... Ganancia;
Beneficio;
Utilidad

Profit sharing ....................... Reparto de las
ganancias

Property ............................... Propiedad

Property insurance ............... Seguro de la propiedad

Proxy.................................... Poder;
Apoderado

Public accountants............... Contadores públicos

Public corporation ............... Corporación pública

Public relations .................... Relaciones públicas

Purchasing ........................... Compras

Quality.................................. Calidad;
Cualidad

| | |
|---|---|
| Quality assurance | Comprobación de calidad |
| Quotas | Cuota |
| Real property | Bienes raíces |
| Recruiting | Reclutamiento |
| Report | Informe |
| Resume | Currículum vitae |
| Retailer | Minorista; Detallista |
| Revenue | Ingresos; Rentas; Entradas |
| Risk | Riesgo |
| Sales promotion | Promoción de ventas |
| Scheduling | Programación |
| Secured loan | Préstamo garantizado |
| Self-insurance | Autoseguro |
| Selling expenses | Gastos de venta |
| Selling point | Argumento de venta |
| Shareholders | Accionistas |
| Small business | Empresa pequeña |
| Sole proprietorship | Dueño único |
| Standards | Patrón; Norma |
| Statistics | Estadística |
| Statutory law | Ley escrita |
| Stock | Acciones |

| | |
|---|---|
| Strategic alliance | Alianza estratégica |
| Supply-chain management | Administración de la cadena de oferta |
| Tariffs | Tarifa; Arancel |
| Team | Equipo |
| Topic | Asunto; Tema |
| Trade allowance | Descuento comercial |
| Trade Show | Exposición comercial |
| Trademark | Marca |
| Unsecured loan | Préstamo sin garantía |
| Unsolicited proposal | Propuesta no solicitada |
| Variable costs | Costos variables |
| Venture capitalist | Capitalista aventurado |
| Voice mail | Correo de voz |
| Wages | Salarios |
| Warehouse | Almacén |
| Warranty | Garantía |
| Wholesalers | Mayoristas |
| World Wide Web | Red mundial |
| Wrongful discharge | Despido injustificado |

# Latin American Holidays

Latin American countries share a list of common holidays. There are also a number of specific holidays for each country.

The common holidays throughout Latin America are:

- January 1: New Year's Day
- Carnival: forty-nine days before Easter—sometimes extended into the preceding week
- May 1: Labor Day
- December 25: Christmas. The period after Christmas is in some places considered vacation until January 2. In some instances, it is even extended to Three Kings on January 6.

The specific holidays for each country are:

### Argentina

May 25: Anniversary of the May Revolution

June 20: Flag Day

July 9: Anniversary of the Argentine Declaration of Independence

July 20: Friend Day

September 11: Teachers' Day

September 21: Spring Day, Students' Day

## Bolivia

June 11: Corpus Christi
July 16: La Paz Day
November 2: All Soul's Day

## Brazil

March 21: Paixão de Cristo
April 21: Tiradentes
Variable dates: Corpus Christi
September 7: Independence Day
October 12: Our Lady Aparecida (patron saint of Brazil), also celebrated as Children's Day
November 2: Finados
November 15: Proclamation of the Republic

## Chile

May 21: Navy Day
June 29: Feast of Saints Peter and Paul
July 16: Our Lady of Mount Carmel
August 15: Assumption of Mary
September 18: Independence Day
September 19: Glories of the Army Day
October 12: Columbus Day
October 31: Reformation Day
November 1: All Saints' Day
December 8: Immaculate Conception Day

## Colombia

January 8: Epiphany
March 19: Saint Joseph's Day
May 21: Ascension Day
Variable dates: Corpus Christi Day

Variable dates (nineteen days after Pentecost): Sacred
  Heart Day
July 2: Feast of Saints Peter and Paul
July 20: Independence Day
August 7: Battle of Boyacá Day
August 15: Assumption Day
October 12: Columbus Day
November 5: All Saints' Day
December 8: Immaculate Conception Day

## Costa Rica

April 11: Battle of Rivas Day
July 25: Guanacaste Day
August 2: Virgen de los Angeles Day
August 15: Mother's Day
September 15: Independence Day
October 12: Meeting of Cultures Day

## Ecuador

June 1: Bridge Public Holiday
May 24: Battle of Pichincha
July 25: Guayaquil Day
August 10: National Day
October 9: Guayaquil Independence Day
November 2: All Souls' Day
November 3: Cuenca Independence Day
December 6: Quito Day

## El Salvador

January 16: La Paz Day
August 3: Fiesta San Salvador
August 4, 5 and 6: Fiestas Patronales

September 15: Independence Day

October 12: Día de la Raza

## Guatemala

April 26: Secretary's Day

May 10: Mother's Day

June 30: Army Day

August 15: Assumption of Mary

September 15: Independence Day

October 20: Revolution Day

November 1: All Saints' Day

## Honduras

February 3: Day of the Virgin of Suyapa

March or April: Good Friday, Easter, Easter Monday

April 14: Day of the Americas

September 10: International Day of the Children

September 15: Independence Day

October 3: Morazán Day

October 12: Columbus Day

October 27: Armed Forces Day

## Mexico

First Monday in February: Día de la Constitución

May 5: Cinco de Mayo

September 16: Día de Independencia (Mexican Independence Day)

November 1–2: Día de Muertos (Day of the Dead)

Third Monday in November: Día de la Revolución

December 12: Our Lady of Guadalupe Day

## Nicaragua

May 30: Mother's Day

July 19: Revolution Day

September 14: San Jacinto Day

September 25: Independence Day

December 8: Immaculate Conception Day

## Panama

January 9: Martyrs' Day (Día de los Mártires)

November 3: Independence (Colombia)

November 5: Independence (Colombia) in Colón

November 10: Grito de Independencia

November 28: Independence (Spain)

## Paraguay

February 3: Día de San Blas

March 1: Cerro Cora

May 15: Independence Day

June 12: Paz del Chaco

August 15: Assumption Day

September 29: Victoria de Boquerón

December 8: Immaculate Conception

## Peru

June 29: Feast of Saints Peter and Paul

July 28, July 29: Independence Day

August 30: Saint Rose of Lima

October 8: Naval Battle of Angamos

November 1: All Saints' Day

December 8: Immaculate Conception Day

## Uruguay

April 19: Landing of the Thirty-Three Orientals

May 18: Battle of Las Piedras

June 19: Birthday of José Gervasio Artigas

July 18: Constitution Day

August 25: Independence Day

## Venezuela

May 30: Mother's Day

July 19: Revolution Day

September 14: San Jacinto Day

September 15: Independence Day

December 8: Immaculate Conception Day

# APPENDIX C

# Bibliography

## Electronic Sources

1. The very first place to research for additional information concerning your destination is *The CIA World Factbook* (www.cia.gov). This is updated biweekly and is accurate and unbiased.

2. The next place to examine is the U.S. Consular Fact Sheets, which can be found at http://travel.state.gov/travel. For each country, there are notes on travel warnings as well as country-specific information. Each country page contains links to a wide variety of accurate information.

3. The World Bank Latin American website (http://go.worldbank.org/F7T4DTVE20) contains numerous articles and links on Latin America that are quite useful. It is here where you will find industry-specific information.

4. The governments of each country also maintain websites for businesspersons considering doing business there. It should not be assumed that this information is unbiased, so cross-checking is in order.

5. A general Internet search for a specific country will be invaluable. If you have access to LexisNexis, this search engine provides a veritable plethora of useful

information. I would also search for the company or
companies you intend to meet. If the site is in Spanish, then utilize an automatic Internet translator,
which will give you a rough approximation of the
text. If you do not have a translation program, there
is adequate software, available for free at a number
of websites, including www.thefreecountry.com.

## Print Sources

What follows is a bibliographic abstract containing relevant books currently in print relating to business in
Latin America, which should be locally available through
a bookstore or your local library.

Mary Murray Bosrock. 1997. *Put Your Best Foot Forward, South America: A Fearless Guide to International
Communication and Behavior.* St. Paul, Minn.: International Education Systems.

Guillermo I. Castillo-Feliu. 2000. *Culture and Customs
of Chile.* Westport, Conn.: Greenwood Press.

Simon Collier, ed. 1992. *The Cambridge Encyclopedia of
Latin American Culture.* New York: Cambridge University Press.

Elizabeth Devine and Nancy L. Braganti. 1988. *The
Travelers' Guide to Latin American Customs and Manners.* New York: St. Martin's Press.

Dean Foster. 2002. *The Global Etiquette Guide to Mexico
and Latin America: Everything You Need to Know for
Business and Travel Success.* New York: J. Wiley &
Sons.

Terri Morrison and Wayne Conway. 1997. *The International Traveler's Guide to Doing Business in Latin America. New York: Macmillan Spectrum.

Joyce Moss and George Wilson. *Peoples of the World, Latin Americans: The Culture, Geographical Setting, and Historical Background of 42 Latin American Peoples.* Detroit: Gale Research.

Judith Noble and Jaime Lacasa. 1991. *The Hispanic Way: Aspects of Behavior, Attitudes, and Customs in the Spanish-Speaking World.* Lincolnwood, Ill.: Passport Books.

Ann Marie Sebath. 2000. *International Business Etiquette, Latin America: What You Need to Know to Conduct Business Abroad with Charm and Savvy.* Franklin Lakes, NJ: Career Press.

Lisa Shaw and Stephanie Dennison. 2005. *Pop Culture Latin America! Media, Arts and Lifestyle.* Santa Barbara, Calif.: ABC-Clio.

Barbara A. Tenenbaum, ed. 1996. *Encyclopedia of Latin American History and Culture*, vol. 5. New York: Scribner's.

Lawrence W. Tuller. 1993. *Doing Business in Latin America and the Caribbean: Including Mexico, The U.S. Virgin Islands and Puerto Rico, Central America, South America.* New York: AMACOM.

Raymond Leslie Williams and Kevin G. Guerrieri. 1999. *Culture and Customs of Colombia.* Westport, Conn.: Greenwood Press.

Donald E. Worcester and Wendell G. Schaeffer. 1971. *The Growth and Culture of Latin America.* New York: Oxford University Press.

# INDEX

Page numbers in **bold** indicate charts or tables.

# ABOUT THE AUTHOR

**Dr. Kevin Diran** received his doctorate from Columbia University and a licentiate in philosophy from Pontifical Gregorian University in Rome. He has spent eight years living, working and teaching in Latin America.

He served as dean at a university in Mexico and taught courses in International Trade. Prior to that he was a licensed customhouse broker and owner/president of Armen Cargo Services in San Francisco, which was an air and ocean international freight forwarder and customhouse broker. The company had offices in San Francisco and Los Angeles, in addition to six others in Latin America and Southeast Asia. He has a distinguished academic career and has held positions as a college vice president, university dean and professor in the United States.

Currently Kevin Diran works as a conference speaker, consultant and writer on topics relating to international commerce.

Kevin Diran lives in Melbourne Beach, Florida, and can be reached for reader comments or clarifications at greenlightdiran@aol.com, or go to his website, www.kevindiran.com, for additional information.